Early Learning Thematic Lesson Plans

32 Thematic Lesson Plans for a Developmentally Appropriate Curriculum

by
Sherrill B. Flora

illustrated by
Julie Anderson

Publisher
Key Education Publishing Company, LLC
Minneapolis, Minnesota

CONGRATULATIONS ON YOUR PURCHASE OF A KEY EDUCATION PRODUCT!

The editors at Key Education are former teachers who bring experience, enthusiasm, and quality to each and every product. Thousands of teachers have looked to the staff at Key Education for new and innovative resources to make their work more enjoyable and rewarding. Key Education is committed to developing educational materials that will assist teachers in building a strong and developmentally appropriate curriculum for young children.

PLAN FOR GREAT TEACHING EXPERIENCES WHEN YOU USE EDUCATIONAL MATERIALS FROM KEY EDUCATION PUBLISHING COMPANY, LLC

This book is dedicated to my "wonderful" husband—who is my best friend, my biggest fan, and my favorite editor! Love You! T, B, & O's!

Credits
Author: Sherrill B. Flora
Inside Illustrations: Julie Anderson
Cover Design: Mary Claire
Editors: George C. Flora
       Bernadette Baczynski
Production: Key Education Staff
Cover Photography: © Comstock
            © Brand X Pictures

Key Education welcomes manuscripts and product ideas from teachers.
For a copy of our submission guidelines, please send a self-addressed, stamped envelope to:
Key Education Publishing Company, LLC
Acquisitions Department
9601 Newton Avenue South
Minneapolis, Minnesota 55431

Standard Book Number:1-933052-07-4
Early Learning Thematic Lesson Plans
Copyright © 2005 by Key Education Publishing Company, LLC
Minneapolis, Minnesota 55431

Introduction

Early Learning Thematic Lesson Plans provides the early childhood teacher with a wealth of information, activities, and well-organized lesson plans for the most popular themes taught in early childhood programs. All the research, planning, and scheduling has been done for you. Open the book, choose a theme, and you can immediately begin teaching.

Although the lesson plans have been written for you, it is highly recommended that the teacher or parent use their own judgement when selecting and introducing various theme-related activities. You are the true expert when it comes to understanding where your children are developmentally. Always remember to adapt or change the activities according to the specific needs and abilities of your children.

The primary focus in *Early Learning Thematic Lesson Plans* was to offer a wide-range of cross-curriculum activities for each thematic unit. The teacher or parent will find: theme-related vocabulary, basic language concepts, child-interactive bulletin boards, music, fingerplays and poetry, stories, science, math, pre-reading, dramatic play, creative art, and cooking experiences woven through the individual thematic units. The last few pages of *Early Learning Thematic Lesson Plans* offers a delightful children's literature reference guide for every thematic unit.

You will also find that many of the themes have reproducible mini-books or activities where "printed words" are provided for the children. The goal here is not to teach reading, but to provide young children with materials that will help create a print-rich environment. Research has proven that young children who are surrounded with words, stories, books, and expressive language will become good readers.

The topics and activities in *Early Learning Thematic Lesson Plans* have been designed to make your lesson planning easier and to engage young learners! This book is a must for everyone who loves working with and teaching young children!

Includes:

❏ Organized lesson plan pages

❏ Popular themes taught in all early childhood programs

❏ Children's literature reference guide

❏ Reproducible patterns and student activity pages

❏ Integrated activities

Contents

Contents

MORNING CIRCLE ACTIVITIES

INTRODUCTION

The first activities of the day are very important to young children. How a teacher chooses to begin each day can greatly influence the children's behavior and their "moods" for the rest of the day. Beginning each day with the same schedule of "Morning Circle" activities will give preschool children a sense of organization and familiarity, and will help prepare them for the rest of the day's upcoming activities.

Morning circle activities can take anywhere from 20 to 30 minutes. During this time the children will be participating in five to six different activities. Providing a variety of activities for the children to do and talk about makes the time pass very quickly and will maintain the interest of the children.

Suggested activities are:

- ❏ Name Recognition
- ❏ Show-and-Tell (Wednesdays)
- ❏ Special News (Fridays)
- ❏ The Weather
- ❏ Today's Helpers
- ❏ The Calendar

NAME RECOGNITION

Name recognition activities will provide the children with the experience of learning to read their own names. The activities may also simply be used for taking attendance.

After using one of the following name recognition ideas, ask the children if anyone is absent and have them speculate why. If a child has returned from an absence, be sure to welcome him back. These types of discussions and questions help the children to feel very important.

1. Photo Cards

Cut pieces of tagboard into four or five-inch squares. Make one square for each child in your class. On each square, tape a photograph of the child on one side of the card, and print the child's name on the other side. Attach yarn at the top so the squares can be hung on a bulletin board.

Each morning ask the children, one at a time, to find their names. If a child chooses correctly, he will turn the card around to discover his own photograph. Rearrange the photographs often so the children are constantly challenged.

(front of card)   *(back of card)*

2. Where Is _____?
(Sung to the tune of "Where is Thumbkin?")

Where is *child's name*?	*(teacher sings)*	How are you today *child's name*?	*(teacher sings)*
Where is *child's name*?	*(teacher sings)*	Very well, I thank you.	*(child sings)*
Here I am.	*(child sings)*	We're glad you're here.	*(everyone sings)*
Here I am.	*(child sings)*	We're glad you're here.	*(everyone sings)*

3. Name Chart

Create a name chart on a large piece of posterboard or cover a bulletin board with brightly colored paper. Write each child's name on an envelope. *(The envelopes will serve as pockets that will hold the children's photographs.)* Attach the envelope to the board with self-stick Velcro™— one side of the Velcro™ on the board and the other side of the Velcro™ on each envelope. This will enable you to rearrange the envelopes often. Make sure when you place the Velcro™ on the board that you leave enough space between the envelopes to accommodate the photographs. *(See illustration.)*

Each of the children will need a photograph of themselves that fits into the envelope. To take attendance have the children place their photo into their name pocket. At the end of the activity the children will be able to see which of their classmates are absent that day.

SHOW-AND-TELL (Wednesdays)

All children love to bring something special to school. From a child's perspective, it is a lot of fun! From a teacher's perspective it can create chaos!

Providing a once-a-week show-and-tell time is a wonderful compromise for the children and the teacher. Giving the children one day to bring a special "something" to school can work extremely well. The children will look forward to this day, and generally put more thought into what they would like to show to their friends. Here are some ideas that will make it easier for you:

1. Ask the parents to put their child's name on each item brought to school. If an item comes unmarked, mark it yourself with removable masking tape.

2. Provide the children with a show-and-tell box. That way the children will know they have a safe place to keep their items until it is time to share them. It is also easier for the teacher to have one place to look for everything that was brought to school that day.

3. Show-and-tell is a wonderful time to help develop expressive language skills. Encourage the children to use descriptive vocabulary and to offer good information. These questions will help guide them: Where did you get it? Who gave it to you? What does it do? Why is it a favorite of yours?

A Special Note About Toys: *If you teach in a child-care center or full-day program with preschoolers who must nap, please allow them to have a special blanket, stuffed animal, or whatever else may help them fall asleep. Something special from home can be a tremendous help!*

SPECIAL NEWS! (FRIDAYS)

Special news is a language experience similar to show-and-tell. In this activity, the children take turns telling about some special event that has taken place or an event that is about to happen. Here are some examples: we are going to grandma's house; we ate dinner at a restaurant; the cat had kittens; mom made my favorite dinner. Remind parents that Friday is "Special News" day, and they should encourage their children to plan what they would like to share.

THE WEATHER

Providing daily weather activities will:

❑ Help children to increase their vocabulary and expressive language skills
❑ Help children to become more aware of their environment
❑ Help children learn to make more appropriate choices of clothing for various weather conditions
❑ Help children learn about the changing seasons

Weather vocabulary:	sun	sunny	cloud	cloudy	thunder	chilly
	rain	rainy	hail	storm	lightening	hot
	snow	wind	windy	cool	cold	warm
	foggy					

1. Weather Wheel

Cut a large circle out of tagboard. Divide the circle into four sections. In each section, draw and color a picture depicting a certain weather condition.

Attach an arrow to the center of the circle using a brass fastener. The daily weather person should move the arrow to the picture showing the day's weather condition. Encourage descriptive vocabulary and ask for a recommendation of what clothing everyone will need to wear for playing outside today.

2. Weather Windows and Weather Warren

Draw a Weather Warren on a large piece of tag board. Place self-stick Velcro™ on the top of his head, shoulders, hands, waist, and feet. Make clothing to fit Warren for various weather conditions.

Make four windows that will be hung on the left side of the bulletin board. On one side of each window, simply draw window panes. On the other side of the window, draw various weather conditions. Attach a string to each window so it can be hung on the bulletin board. The children will leave the correct window showing and turn around the other windows. With this display you can use two weather people: one to dress Warren and one to change the weather windows.

3. Weather Felt Hanging

The weather felt hanging provides the children with the experience of adding felt pieces to make a flannel board picture of the day's weather. The children will also be able to add seasonal accents, such as flowers, leaves, and whatever additional pieces the teacher would like to make.

You can also use the hanging to show the children what other parts of the country may look like. For example, if you live in southern Florida you can show the children a picture of a snowy day.

The background of the wall hanging is made from light blue felt. Glue a strip of green felt at the bottom to represent grass. Cut a piece of white felt the same size that can be added for snow. Glue a brown tree trunk with branches. Additional pieces may be made for depicting different weather conditions. Here are some sample patterns:

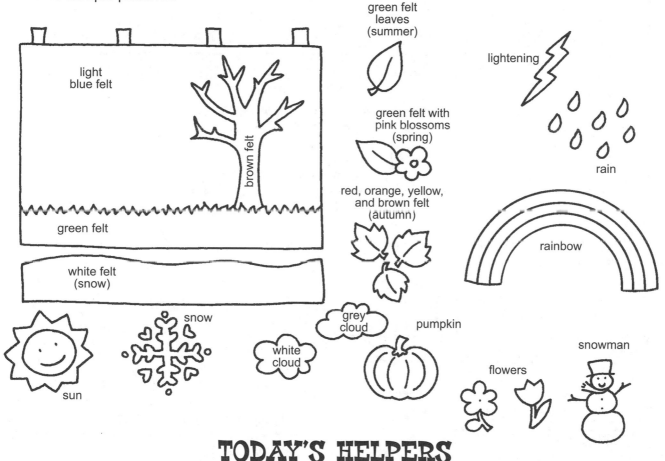

TODAY'S HELPERS

The following are ideas for posting classroom helpers. These duties are meant to be changed daily. Changing the jobs on a daily basis will allow the children to have turns more frequently and will lessen the amount of time each child must wait for a favorite job.

1. Helping Hands Job Assignment

Trace each child's hand on tagboard, cut out, and print the child's name on the palm. On a large piece of tagboard make pockets and pictures for each classroom job. The hands will fit into the pockets. Attach a larger envelope to the chart for storing all of the hands. Keep up all year as the job assignment chart.

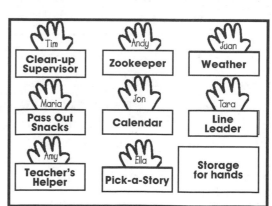

2. Our Helpers

Make a paper doll shape for each boy and girl in your class. Let the children finish the dolls by coloring in facial features, clothes, and gluing on yarn for hair. This activity can also be done by having the children make stick puppets of themselves using tongue depressors. Make job cards that can be placed under the children's figures to show who has what responsibility for the day.

THE CALENDAR

Daily calendar activities will give the children opportunities to:

- ❑ Increase rote counting skills
- ❑ Learn the days of the week
- ❑ Learn the months of the year
- ❑ Increase number recognition skills
- ❑ Begin associating which holiday falls within which month
- ❑ Build sequencing and patterning skills

Make a large calendar from tagboard and laminate it for durability. *(Commerically made calendars may also be purchased.)*

Month

Sunday	Monday	Tuesday	Wednesday	Thursday	Friday	Saturday

Days of the Week Wheel

A "Days of the Week Wheel" is a fun addition to keep on display with your calendar activities. Have the children turn the arrow until they have found the correct day. For young preschoolers, add pictures of special things that you do on each day, such as show-and-tell on Wednesdays.

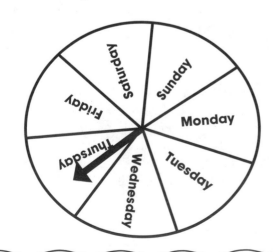

Monthly Calendar Patterns

Monthly patterns can be found on pages 11 and 12. Reproduce these patterns on colored construction paper. Number each one and laminate them so they may be used over and over again.

Monthly Calendar Patterns

September

October

November

December

January

February

March

April

May

June

July

August

32 Weekly Thematic Lesson Plans

Theme 1: Great News! School Begins! (Getting Acquainted!)

	Activity 1	Activity 2	Activity 3	Activity 4
Monday	**DISCUSSION TOPIC: WELCOME TO SCHOOL** Welcome the children back to school. Talk about being good friends. Let the children explore the classroom. Help the children learn where everything is kept. (Send letter home to parents. See page 15.)	**TOUR OF THE SCHOOL** Take your class on a tour of the school building. Children feel more secure when they are familiar with their surroundings.	**TAKE MY PICTURE** Use a Polaroid or digital camera to take pictures of all the children in the class. Frame the pictures on bright construction paper. Fold the corners so the construction paper looks like a real frame. Hang in a classroom photo gallery.	**INSTANT PUDDING** Make instant pudding using the "shaker" method. (Follow the directions on the box.) Let each child have a turn shaking the pudding in a large container. Each child can make their own pudding by pouring the pudding from the large container into baby food jars.
Tuesday	**DISCUSSION TOPIC: GETTING ACQUAINTED** Encourage children to talk to their parents about school. Find out who remembers the teachers' name. Friends' names? Ask which of yesterdays activities was the most fun. Provide parents with daily information, post the "What We Did Today" chart near your classroom. (See page 16.)	**TELEPHONE** Use real phones if possible. Set up two "homes" or "offices" out of sight of each other. Children can face away from each other or sit behind a screen. The children can introduce themselves over the phone, guess who is talking, and learn proper phone etiquette.	**FOLLOW THE LEADER** One of the best group movement activities is "Follow the Leader." Children love this game! It is a comfortable way for children to get to know each other. Make sure everyone gets a chance to be the leader. (And remember—it is more fun when played with music.)	**MATCH THE LOLLIPOPS** Make lollipops out of construction paper and craft sticks. Cut out construction paper circles, tape to the craft sticks, and put a sticker on the circle. (**Make two identical sets.**) Pass out one set to the children and keep the other set. Hold up one lollipop and the child with the matching lollipop holds up theirs.
Wednesday	**SHOW-AND-TELL WEDNESDAY** **DISCUSSION TOPIC: REMEMBERING NAMES** Ask the children if they can say the name of the person sitting next to them. Who can remember the names of five children in our class? Play "Duck, Duck, Goose" to help children learn names.	**ONE, TWO, THREE** One, two, three. One, two, three. How many children Make one, two, three? ____ and ____ and ____ Make three. Please come and stand In front of me. (Use the names of all the children in the class.)	**MIRROR, MIRROR ON THE WALL** Have each child choose a partner. One child is the mirror and the other child is pretending to look in the mirror. The child who is the mirror must imitate all of the movements and facial expressions made by the child looking in the mirror.	**LOLLIPOPS AND A NEW GAME** Use the lollipops that were made for yesterday's activity. This time pass out all of the lollipops to the children. Have the children walk around the room to find the matching lollipop. (Lollipops can also be made for numbers, colors, shapes, and alphabet letters.)
Thursday	**DISCUSSION TOPIC: LET'S LEARN ABOUT EACH OTHER** Make a classroom growth chart. It can be a large ruler, tree, etc. Measure all the children and write their names by their heights. Who is the tallest? Shortest? Play a name guessing game.	**MY STORY** Have the children dictate a short story about themselves. Have the children illustrate their stories and share them with the class. Use the story template found on page 18.	**THIS IS MY TEACHER** Use the reproducible page "My Teacher," found on page 17 to complete this activity. Children love to draw pictures of their teachers. Have the children draw your picture and bring their drawings home to share with their parents. It is a great way to encourage children to tell their parents about school.	**WHO DO YOU SEE?** Ask the children, one at a time, to stand in front of a full-length mirror. Ask each child to identify body parts and point to them in the mirror. It is also fun to cover half the mirror with paper and have the children talk about the body parts that they cannot see.
Friday	**SPECIAL NEWS FRIDAY** **DISCUSSION TOPIC: IT WAS A FUN WEEK!** Ask the children what they liked best about this week. What activities would they like to do next week? Repeat a favorite activity.	**I'M THINKING** Ask the children to look around the room and silently choose someone that they would like to describe. For example: "I see a girl with a red bow. This girl has brown eyes." The teacher should describe someone first and then let the children all take turns trying to describe someone.	**I AM A GOOD FRIEND** This activity makes a fun display. Tape a construction paper circle (skin tone) on a craft stick. Each child should make the face look like them. Use yarn, markers, buttons, sequins, and crayons. Each child should complete the sentence, "I am a good friend, because . . ." and post it under their picture.	**KNOCK, KNOCK. WHO'S THERE?** A child ("it") stands blindfolded (or wears sunglasses) with his or her back to the class. The teacher taps another child. The other child says "Knock, knock." "It" responds, "Who's there?" and tries to guess who was knocking.

 Early Learning Thematic Lesson Plans

Dear Parents,

Welcome to preschool! This will be an exciting year for both you and your child. Let's begin the year by helping each other. You can help me by answering the questions at the bottom of the page. Please return as soon as possible.

Here are some ideas that will help you and your child adjust to the new routine of school.

1. Talk positively about school. Stress the fun of new friends and activities. If your child sees that you like school, your child will be more apt to develop positive feelings about school, too.
2. Always reassure your child that you will be back at the end of the day. By saying something as simple as, "Have fun, I'll be back soon, and you can tell me about all the things you did today," you can make the transition of your leaving much easier.
3. Let your child bring a "security-something" to school. A special blanket or stuffed animal can offer much comfort.
4. During the first few days of school, plan to stay a few extra moments. Do not rush out the door.
5. And finally, even if your child is tearful, keep the good-bye cheerful!

I am looking forward to an exciting year.

Your child's teacher,

-------------------------------------- ALL ABOUT MY CHILD --------------------------------------

My child's name: _____

1. Does your child have any brothers or sisters? _____

2. Do you have any pets? If so, list the types of animals and their names._____
_____

3. Does your child have a special blanket or other security item? When is it most often used?_____
_____

4. What are your child's favorite toys, activities, and games? _____
_____

5. Does your child have any special fears? (e.g., clowns, thunderstorms, things that might happen while your child is at school) _____

6. Does your child have any special stories or books? _____

7. Please use the back of the paper to provide me with any extra information that you think will help me better understand your child.

Thank you so much. This information will help me get to know your child quickly! I am looking forward to a wonderful school year!

Date: _____

This is what we did today?

_____

_____

_____

_____

_____

_____

I had a Great Day! Ask me about it!

My teacher is proud of me because:

_____

_____

_____

_____

_____

_____

Signed, _____

MY TEACHER

Illustrated by _____

My teacher's name is _____.

My teacher likes me because _____.

This is me!

My name is _____.

Theme 2: These People Belong to Me! (Families)

	Activity 1	Activity 2	Activity 3	Activity 4
Monday	**DISCUSSION TOPIC: FAMILIES ARE SPECIAL** This week the children will be learning about families. Explain that families are special. What are some things that you do as a family? Who are some of the people in your family? Ask the children to bring pictures of their families to share at morning circle tomorrow. *(Send home note, found on page 20.)*	**WHO LIVES AT MY HOUSE?** Using a dollhouse and a variety of dolls, begin a discussion of home and the people that live there. Let each child have a turn placing all of their family members in the house. Do not forget to prepare dolls who can be grandparents and pets. Who is the tallest? Shortest? Youngest? Oldest?	**CUT AND PASTE FAMILY** Have the children cut out pictures from old magazines and paste them on construction paper. Ask the children to find pictures of people who look like parents, grandparents, brothers, sisters, etc. Have the children share the pictures they cut out with the class.	**SIDEWALK GAMES** Complete directions can be found on page 22.
Tuesday	**DISCUSSION TOPIC: THIS IS MY FAMILY** Today the children will share their family pictures. Bring a picture of your own family to share, too. Talk about siblings. Who has brothers? Sisters? Pets? Babies at home?	**THAT'S ME** This finger play can be found on page 22. **FAMILY SCRAPBOOK** Send home the parent letter found on page 20.	**FAMILY SCRAPBOOK CONTINUED** Continue working on the family scrapbook that was started yesterday.	**FARMER IN THE DELL** Have the children sing and act out, "The Farmer in the Dell." Discuss with the children that this song is about a family. Use the patterns found on pages 21 and 22 to make stick puppets or flannel board characters.
Wednesday	**SHOW-AND-TELL WEDNESDAY** **DISCUSSION TOPIC: GRANDPARENTS** Talk about grandparents. What are some special things that you like to do with your grandparents? What makes your grandparents special?	**THESE ARE GRANDMOTHER'S GLASSES** This finger play can be found on page 22.	**SPECIAL PAINTINGS FOR MY GRANDPARENTS** Brush buttermilk on manila paper and then let the children use colored chalk on top of the wet milk. This is an interesting medium for chalk drawings. The children's grandparents will love the special gift.	**FAMILY FAVORITES** Ask the children about the songs that their families sing or listen to at home. Take turns singing some of the favorite songs of each child's family. The children may also wish to sing, "The Farmer in the Dell" again.
Thursday	**DISCUSSION TOPIC: PETS ARE PART OF A FAMILY** Talk about pets. In many families, pets are important family members. What are some of the things that people must do to take care of their pets? Besides food and water, pets need love and attention, just like people!	**WHO IS MISSING?** Use dolls or pictures of people to represent family members. Take four or five people and show them to the children. Have the children close their eyes. While their eyes are covered, remove one person. Ask the children to guess who is missing.	**FAMILY TAG** Play a game of tag. To avoid being tagged by the person who is "it," a child must sit down and call out the name of a family member. This is challenging for a preschooler. No one is tagged "out" of the game. The child tagged gets to be the next "it."	**WALK WITH A ROPE** Take the children outside for a walk. You may wish to teach the children how to walk together while holding a rope. Take this opportunity to discuss safety and the importance of staying together. What are their parent's rules about safety and staying together when outside or away from home?
Friday	**SPECIAL NEWS FRIDAY** **DISCUSSION TOPIC: FAMILY IS IMPORTANT** Talk about responsibilities and chores. Everyone in a family must help. What do you do to help around your house?	**BIG AND LITTLE** Find many objects in your classroom and have the children describe them as big or little. Then talk about people in the family. Who is big and who is little?	**WHAT DO MOMMY AND DADDY DO AT WORK?** Collect old clothes and props *(shoes, hats, coats, briefcases, office supplies, etc.)* that can be used for playing dress-up. Encourage a play session of dressing up like mommy or daddy at work. *(Use these items to establish a permanent dress-up corner.)*	**ROLE PLAY** Choose several children to play the parts of different family members. Give the "family" different situations to role play: dinner, bedtime, grocery shopping, etc.

This week we are learning about families!

Dear Parents,

This week our theme is **"These people belong to me!"** Please send a family photograph to school with your child tomorrow. During morning circle time, the children will be sharing their family pictures with the rest of the class and telling some things about their families.

Please help prepare your child. Look at the picture together. Talk about all of the people in the photo. What are their names? Are they grandparents? Aunts? Uncles? Cousins? Parents? Brothers? Sisters? Pets? When was the picture taken? Where were you?

We will take very good care of the photos. They will be returned at the end of the day. Thank you for your assistance.   Sincerely,

_____

Date: *Your child's teacher*

- -

We want to make family scrapbooks!

Dear Parents,

We need your help! The children are going to be making family scrapbooks as part of our thematic study of families. We are asking that you choose 8 to 10 special family photos and make black and white photocopies of them. Most color photographs will copy nicely as a black and white photocopy.

The children will take the photocopies of the pictures and use them to create their own family scrapbook. This wonderful project is sure to become a family treasure!

_____

Date: *Your child's teacher*

Farmer in the Dell Patterns

Copy, color, and cut out the patterns below. Back with self-stick Velcro™ to use on the flannel board, attach a craft stick for creating stick puppets, or use the patterns to make a songbook for each child.

Farmer

Wife

Child

Dog

Nurse

Farmer in the Dell Patterns (continued)

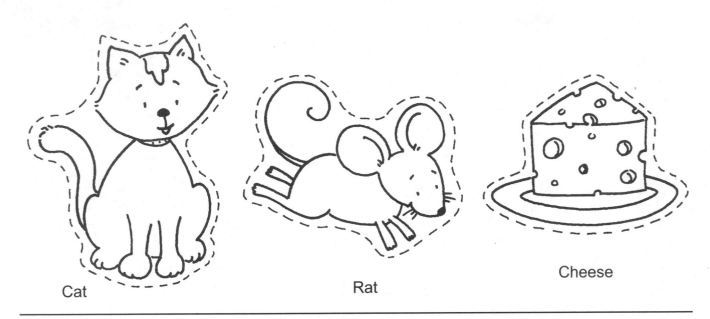

Cat   Rat   Cheese

THESE ARE GRANDMOTHER'S GLASSES

These are grandmother's glasses.   *(Make circles around each eye with fingers.)*
This is grandmother's cap.   *(Hold fingers interlocked over your head.)*
This is the way she folds her hands   *(Fold hands.)*
And lays them in her lap.   *(Lay hands in lap.)*

THAT'S ME

This is me, I'd like you to meet   *(Bow.)*
I have one little head and two little feet.   *(Shake head, then feet.)*
I have two little arms and one little nose,   *(Hold up arms, then touch nose.)*
And ten little fingers and ten little toes!   *(Wiggle fingers and toes.)*

SIDEWALK GAMES

Discarded window shades or plastic tablecloths can make great surfaces for creating indoor sidewalk games. Cut the plastic into strips that can be taped together to make a long indoor sidewalk. Divide the sidewalk into squares. Prepare different things to put in the squares, such as shapes, colors, animals, alphabet letters, etc. The children can walk along the sidewalk and name the things they are stepping on.

The children can also throw beanbags onto the sidewalk, naming the things that appear on the squares where the beanbags land.

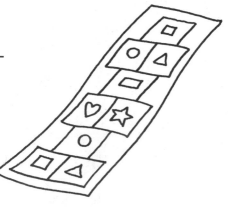

Theme 3: Where Do You Live? (Homes)

	Activity 1	Activity 2	Activity 3	Activity 4
Monday	**DISCUSSION TOPIC: HOMES** Tell the children that this week they are going to talk about different types of homes. What are the names of some of the rooms in a home? Name some things that you can find in each room.	**THE THREE LITTLE PIGS** Read the children the story of "The Three Little Pigs." Small children adore this story. Talk about the types of homes that the pigs built. Which house would they like? What other materials could they use to build a house? Use the pattern on page 27 for retelling the story.	**LET'S PLAY HOUSE** Cover the tables and chairs with sheets and blankets. Let the children help create some wonderful tent homes. Large appliance boxes make great playhouses. Painted and decorated, they can become a permanent addition to your classroom.	**I LIVE NEXT TO YOU** Talk about neighbors. Can the children name some of their neighbors? Place two chairs side by side. Choose one child to sit on a chair, then let that child choose a friend to sit on the other chair. Encourage the children to say, "I live 'next to' you." Each child should have a turn.
Tuesday	**DISCUSSION TOPIC: SOME PEOPLE LIVE IN APARTMENTS** Talk about apartments. Often just one family lives in a house, but many different families live in an apartment building. Does anyone in our class live in an apartment? Do you know who lives next door to you? Across the hall?	**MANY/FEW WINDOWS** Complete directions can be found on page 24.	**BUILDING BLOCKS** Using building blocks, have the children build houses and apartment buildings. **Great idea:** If you do not have many large building blocks, collect half-gallon milk cartons. When covered in contact paper they make wonderful building blocks.	**WHO IS IN THE APARTMENT?** Using a very large sheet of paper, draw the outline of an apartment building with many windows. Tape it to the wall. Have the children cut out pictures of people from old magazines and paste them in the windows. This will help the children visualize the concept of "many."
Wednesday	**SHOW-AND-TELL WEDNESDAY** **DISCUSSION TOPIC: WHERE DO YOU LIVE?** Discuss with the children how important it is to know their addresses. They can always find their way home if they know where they live. Make a graph to record how many children know their address.	**THIS IS MY ADDRESS** Use the reproducible activity found on page 25. Encourage the parents to help their children learn their addresses and phone numbers.	**THE INCOMPLETE HOUSE** Give each child a copy of "Finish The House," found on page 26. Suggest some of the things that they might wish to add to their homes. Then let the children complete their homes. This activity will give you some insight on the children's fine motor maturity.	**CRAFT STICK HOUSE** Give each child craft sticks or tongue depressors. Have the children paste the sticks in the shape of a house. Windows and doors can be added when the paste is dry.
Thursday	**DISCUSSION TOPIC: MANY DIFFERENT HOMES** Set up a library table with several books about homes and where people live. Give the children time to examine the books. Let each child find a favorite house in one of the books and share it with the class.	**TALL AND SHORT HOMES** Find many pictures of houses and apartment buildings. Have the children sort the pictures according to whether the buildings are tall or short.	**SOAP FLAKES FINGER PAINT** This recipe can be found on page 24. Have the children use the finger paint to draw their homes.	**FIND MY HOUSE** Choose one child to be "it." "It" covers his or her eyes. Another child hides and whispers, "come and find my house." "It" must find the hidden child. The child who is "it" chooses another child to be "it" and then gets a turn to be the hidden child.
Friday	**SPECIAL NEWS FRIDAY** **DISCUSSION TOPIC: NEIGHBORHOOD** Let the children create a neighborhood/home mural. Place a large sheet of paper on a wall or bulletin board. Let each child paint a house on the paper.	**TWO LITTLE HOUSES** This finger play can be found on page 24.	**BULLETIN BOARD CITY** Complete directions can be found on page 24.	**BULLETIN BOARD CITY CONTINUED** Finish the work on the bulletin board city that was started yesterday.

MANY/FEW WINDOWS

On a large sheet of construction paper, draw a small square to represent a house and a tall rectangle to represent an apartment building. Prepare many white construction paper windows for the children to glue onto the house and apartment building. Talk about that there are a "few" windows on a house and "many" windows in an apartment building.

Use other materials found in your classroom to visually demonstrate the concept of "few" and "many," such as children, blocks, or pieces of cereal.

TWO LITTLE HOUSES

Two little houses, closed up tight,   *(Make two closed fists.)*
Open the windows, and let in the light. *(Spread hands apart as if opening a window.)*
Ten little people stand tall and straight, *(Hold up ten fingers.)*
Ready for school to start at eight.   *(Use fingers to make a running motion.)*

SOAP FLAKES FINGER PAINT

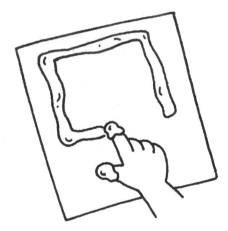

You will need: Soap flakes *(Ivory Snow™ detergent works well),* water, and tempera paint or food coloring.

Directions: Beat the soap flakes in a small amount of water until the mixture has the consistency of whipped cream. Add tempera paint or food coloring and mix well. This type of finger paint may be used on a smooth tabletop or finger painting paper.

Encourage the children to draw houses with the paint, using triangles, rectangles, and squares in their designs.

BULLETIN BOARD CITY

Cover a large bulletin board with white paper. Let the children (with your guidance) draw streets.

Then have the children cut out pictures of houses and buildings. The real estate section of the newspaper is a wonderful resource for this activity. Paste the pictures on the bulletin board paper.

Finally, have the children add trees, cars, and people to the city. Each child should choose a house on the bulletin board to be his or her very own. Add a tiny mailbox next to the house with the child's name on it.

This Is My Address

Print your address on the mailbox.

Finish the House

Draw and color furniture and people.

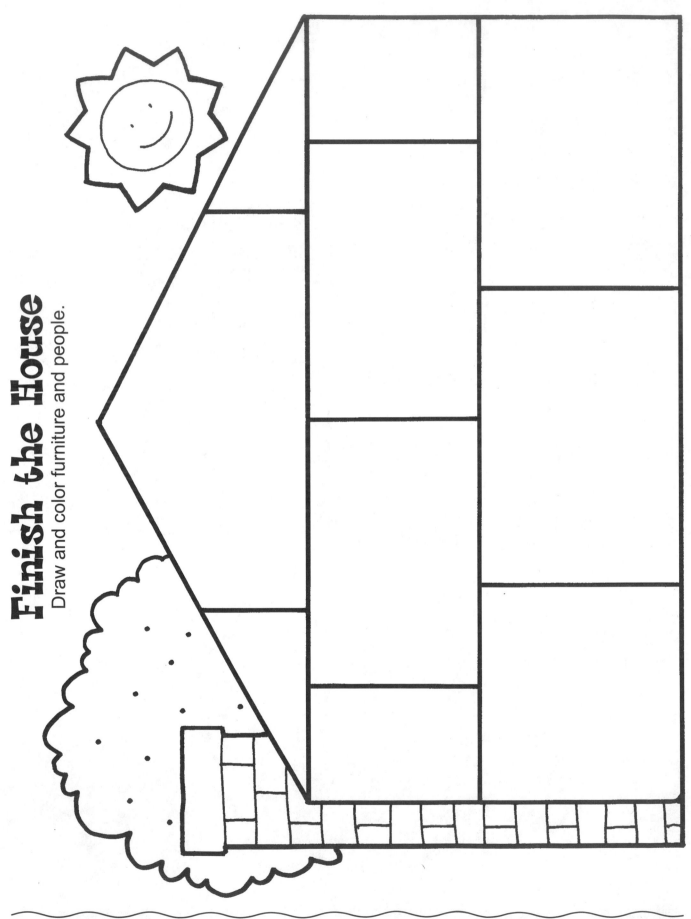

The Three Little Pigs Patterns

Copy onto card stock, color, and cut out the patterns. Attach craft sticks to make stick puppets, self-stick Velcro™ to use on the flannel board, or self-stick magnetic strips to use on a magnetic board.

Theme 4: Apples! Apples! Apples! (Beginning the School Year)

	Activity 1	Activity 2	Activity 3	Activity 4
Monday	**DISCUSSION TOPIC: APPLES** Tell the children that this week they are going to learn all about apples. In many places, apples are at their best in late September. Where do apples grow? What color are apples?	**PAINT APPLES** On a wall or bulletin board make a large tree out of brown and green construction paper. Have each child paint the back of a small paper plate the color red and paste a stem and two leaves on the top. *(See the next activity for displaying the apples.)*	**UP AND DOWN ON THE APPLE TREE** Ask the children one at a time where they wish to place their red paper plate apples on the tree. Should they go "up" on the green part of the tree, or should the apples go "down" on the ground?	**LET'S MAKE BAKED APPLE DUMPLINGS** The recipe for baked apple dumplings can be found on page 29.
Tuesday	**DISCUSSION TOPIC: APPLE ART** If possible, arrange a field trip to a local apple orchard. Send home permission notes and a request for parent volunteer chaperones.	**CUT-AND-PASTE APPLE TREE** The reproducible "Cut-and-Paste Apple Tree" activity can be found on page 31.	**APPLE PRINTS** Prepare bowls of red paint and cut several apples in half. Have the children use a paintbrush to apply the paint on the apples and then make apple prints on white paper. When the paint is dry, the children can add brown stems and green leaves. These projects can make nice place mats.	**LARGE APPLE PATTERN** The large apple pattern found on page 30, can be used for a variety of activities. Teach the color red and let the children color the apple. Add lines and use as creative writing paper. It can also be used as note-paper for newsletters and for notes home to parents.
Wednesday	**SHOW-AND-TELL WEDNESDAY** **DISCUSSION TOPIC: APPLES ARE A FRUIT** An apple is a fruit. There are many different kinds of fruits. Ask the children to help you make a list of all the fruits that they can think of. Take a poll of their favorite fruits and make a graph.	**APPLESAUCE** The recipe for applesauce can be found on page 29.	**MATCHING APPLE FACES** Prepare ten apple drawings – give each apple a different face. Make another identical set so there are 20 apple drawings in all. Mix up the apples on a table and let the children enjoy trying to find the matching pairs.	**PLAYDOUGH APPLES** The recipe for playdough apples can be found on page 29.
Thursday	**DISCUSSION TOPIC: APPLE RED** Ask the children if anyone is wearing red today. Announce that tomorrow will be Red Day. Everyone should wear something red. *(Post this announcement on your parents notification board or be sure to send a note home.)*	**I'M A LITTLE APPLE** Sung to the tune of *"I'm a Little Teapot."* You can find the words on page 29.	**JOHNNY APPLESEED** Read the children the story of *Johnny Appleseed*. If you do not know the story or have the book, a version of the story is easily found on the internet by simply searching for "Johnny Appleseed."	**BOBBING FOR APPLES** Now this will be messy but tons of fun! Fill a big bucket with water and let the children try to bob for apples. *(Be sure to ask parents to send an extra shirt to school today!)*
Friday	**SPECIAL NEWS FRIDAY** **DISCUSSION TOPIC: IT'S RED DAY** Today is red day. Give each child an opportunity to show the class what he or she is wearing that is red. Be prepared for families who forget. Have red scarves, hats, etc., on hand to share.	**COUNTING APPLE SEEDS** Use the large apple pattern on page 29 or make your own smaller apples. Each child will make an apple seed counting book. On the first apple, print a "1" and draw one seed. On the second apple, print a "2" and draw two seeds, and so on. Staple the apples together to make a counting book.	**APPLE TASTING** Bring in a couple of red apples, green apples, and yellow apples. Cut into small pieces and have an apple tasting party. Make a graph of the colors and chart which the children liked best. Can you tell from the chart which color the children liked the least? Draw conclusions.	**TEN APPLES UP ON TOP** Read the book, *Ten Apples Up On Top* by Theo LeSeig (Dr. Seuss). Let the children try walking around the room with beanbags on their heads, just like in the story.

BAKED APPLE DUMPLINGS

Discuss apples with the children. Ask them, "What do you think we can make with apples?" Most children will say applesauce. They may be surprised when you tell them apple dumplings!

You will need: 2 pie crust sticks *(or an other type of ready-to-bake pie crust dough),* 8 unpeeled apples, 4 cups sugar, 4 teaspoons cinnamon, and 4 teaspoons butter.

Directions: Roll out the pie crust sticks and cut them into squares. Four squares for each pie stick. Using a knife, dig out the core of a whole apple. *(Do this step yourself.)* After covering the bottom of the apple with the dough, fill the hole with sugar, cinnamon, and butter. Finish wrapping the apple in one square of the pie crust dough. Pinch the dough together at the top. Repeat for the remaining apples. Bake at 350° for 45 minutes. Let cool and divide for the children to eat. Yum!

APPLESAUCE

Talk about this activity with the children a day or so before you plan to cook. Ask each child to bring an apple from home. The children will love helping by being responsible for some of the ingredients.

You will need: (Adjust this recipe according to how many children you have in your class.) 6 apples, 1/2 cup water, 1 cup sugar, 1 teaspoon cinnamon, and, for extra fun, a few hot cinnamon candies to add a splash of color and a hint of added flavor.

Directions: Peel, core, and cut the apples. Put in a saucepan. Add the water, sugar, and cook until the apples are soft. Another great food treat!

PLAYDOUGH APPLES

Children love playing with playdough, and it is even more fun when they get to make the dough all by themselves! Here is a successful recipe to try.

You will need: Red food coloring, 1 cup water, 1 cup salt, 1 cup flour, 6 teaspoons alum, and 2 tablespoons salad oil.

Directions: Add the food coloring to the water. Place all of the ingredients in a large mixing bowl. Mix until the consistency is smooth and firm. The playdough will last for several weeks if it is stored in an airtight container. Show the children how to roll a ball with the playdough. The children can make playdough apples.

I'M A LITTLE APPLE
(Sung to the tune of "I'm A Little Teapot")

I'm a little apple,	*(Hold arms at side.)*
Round and red.	*(Use arms to form a big circle.)*
Here are my leaves,	*(Touch top of head with both hands.)*
Here is my stem.	*(Touch head with one hand.)*
When I finish growing,	*(Hold arms at side.)*
Round and red.	*(Use arms to form a big circle.)*
I fall from the tree and	*(Pretend to start falling.)*
Land on my head!	*(Fall down.)*

Large Apple Pattern

Use with the activity ideas found on page 28.

Cut-and-Paste Apple Tree

Directions: Teach the children the rhyme. Ask the children to color the tree and the apples, then draw a smiley face on each apple. Then have them cut out the tree and the apples, and paste the apples on the tree. Send the completed trees home with the children so they can share the rhyme with their parents.

The Apple Tree

Way up in the apple tree,
Two little apples smiled at me.
I shook that tree,
As hard as I could.
Down they came.
Yum, they were good!

Theme 5: Who Works in Your Neighborhood? (Community Helpers)

	Activity 1	Activity 2	Activity 3	Activity 4
Monday	**DISCUSSION TOPIC: FIREFIGHTERS** This week the children are going to learn about some of the people who work in the community and our neighbor-hoods. They are called community helpers. Can you name some community helpers? The first community helper we will learn about is the firefight-er—a hero!	**WHAT WOULD YOU DO IF . . .** Ask the children what they know about firefighters. After 9/11 many children know a lot! Make a list of all the things they know. Use the question guide found on page 33 to complete the rest of this activity.	**MAKE FIREFIGHTER HATS** A reproducible firefighter hat can be found on page 34. **LADDER ON THE FLOOR** Using masking tape, make a ladder on the floor. Have the children walk on the sides of the ladder and on the rungs by walking forwards, backwards, and on tiptoes. This activity increases balance without the danger of falling off the ladder.	**I DON'T PLAY WITH MATCHES** Teach the children the song, *"I Don't Play with Matches"* found on page 33. **STOP, DROP, AND ROLL** Teach the children that they should stop, drop, and roll when they smell smoke. Practice!
Tuesday	**DISCUSSION TOPIC: BUS DRIVERS & MAIL CARRIERS** Today the children are going to talk about two community help-ers: bus drivers and mail car-riers. Has anyone ever ridden a bus? What are some of the things that a bus driver must know? How do you behave on a bus? What are some things that a mail carrier does?	**THE BUS STOP GAME** Directions for this game can be found on page 33. **MAKE A SCHOOL BUS** Use the bus pattern on page 35. Copy the pattern for each child. Have the children color the buses. Look through old magazines for faces. Have the children cut out the faces and paste a face in each window.	**LET'S GET MAIL!** Have each child bring a shoe box to school. Decorate and print the child's name on each box. Provide the children with paper, envelopes, and stick-ers. Let them have the fun of "writing" *(coloring pictures)*, putting them in envelopes, adding sticker stamps and delivering their mail.	**LETTER DICTATION** Have the children dictate postcards that can actually be sent in the mail. *(Ask parents to donate the stamps.)* The children will be thrilled when their postcards arrive at home.
Wednesday	**SHOW-AND-TELL WEDNESDAY** **DISCUSSION TOPIC: SANITATION ENGINEERS** Who knows what a sanitation engineer does? Any guesses? Most children call this person the garbage man. What would happen if we did not have sanitation engineers?	**DON'T BE A LITTERBUG!** What is a litterbug? Talk about the importance of keeping our environment clean. What is recycling? Provide bottles, paper, and plastic and let the children sort them into the proper categories. Go on a walk around the school and pick up any trash!	**TRASH TOSS** (two versions) Play a game similar to basket-ball in the classroom. You will need two wastepaper baskets and some "clean trash" (pa-per). Let the children crumble the paper and toss it in the wastepaper basket from a distance. This game can also be played as a relay race; two lines, two baskets, and two piles of crumbled paper.	**OSCAR THE GROUCH!** Oscar is famous for his love of trash. On page 36 you will find a reproducible pattern of a trash can. Have the children draw a picture of Oscar in the can. Torn paper and other 'trash' can be glued around the can. (This should make Oscar very happy!)
Thursday	**DISCUSSION TOPIC: POLICE OFFICERS** Today the children are going to discuss the work of police officers. Be sure to let the children know when you are discussing all the community helpers that both men and women can perform all of the community helper jobs.	**POLICE OFFICER PUPPETS** Have each child cut out a man or woman's face from a magazine. Glue the face to the top of a tongue depres-sor. Then cut out a hat from blue construction paper and paste it to the top of the head. Use these puppets when the children learn the rhyme "Five Strong Police Officers" found on page 33.	**FIVE STRONG POLICE OFFICERS** This rhyme can be found on page 33. Have the children use the puppets from yester-day to dramatize this rhyme in groups of five.	**RED LIGHT/GREEN LIGHT** This is a fun, traditional game with a police twist. A child plays the role of the police officer. All of the other children stand in a line. When the officer says, "green light," the children may move forward. When the officer says, "red light," the children must stop.
Friday	**SPECIAL NEWS FRIDAY** **DISCUSSION TOPIC: GROCERS** Today the children are going to talk about the grocer and gro-cery stores. Where does our food come from? How does it get to the grocery store? What are some of the things that a grocer does?	**GROCERY STORE COLLAGES** Give the children a variety of newspapers and magazines where they can find pictures of different foods. Let them cut out the foods and paste them on construction paper.	**OUR GROCERY STORE** This creative play corner can become a permanent play area in your classroom. Collect (and clean) cartons, containers, boxes, and cans. Place a cash register, butcher paper, shopping bags, and a shopping cart in the play center. The children will have hours of fun grocery shopping!	**COMMUNITY HELPERS BULLETIN BOARD** Divide your bulletin board into sections—one section for each community helper. Display pictures and objects that represent each job. Ask children to bring things from home. Make this a family project.

QUESTION GUIDE FOR, "WHAT WOULD YOU DO IF . . . "

Discuss with the children how fire can be very dangerous but also helpful. It is important for us to learn about fire so that we can appreciate how it can help and how it can hurt.

Discuss some of the good things about fire. People use fire to heat their homes and to cook. Fire is also used in factories, and for cooking over campfires when we are camping.

Now discuss some of the ways that fire can be harmful. For example, it can burn us. Only adults who know a lot about fire should build a fire or use matches. Play, "What would you do if..."

1. You see a fire down the street.
2. You see a child playing with matches.
3. You smell smoke in the house.
4. You see a fire in your backyard.
5. You see children with candles.

I DON'T PLAY WITH MATCHES
(Sung to the tune of "I'm a Little Teapot")
I don't play with matches, no sirree!
Because I know, they don't belong to me.
I don't play with matches. Neither should you!
Fire can burn things and me too!

THE BUS STOP GAME

This game is played like "Follow the Leader." Put on some music. Choose one child to be the driver. Scatter the children all around the room. When the music plays, the driver begins to move as if he or she is driving the bus. When the music stops, the driver must stop. The child closest to the driver gets on the bus and holds the waist of the driver. The music begins again and the two children move together. The game continues until all of the children have gotten on the bus.

FIVE STRONG POLICE OFFICERS

Five strong police officers run through the station door.
One jumped into his car, and then there were four.

Four strong police officers take care of kids like me.
One walked a child home, and then there were three.

Three strong police officers protect me and you.
One stopped some traffic, and now there were two.

Two strong police officers—look how fast they can run!
One caught a bad guy and now there was one.

One strong police officer pointed to the top.
He reminded the cars that they all had to stop.

(Enlarge and make five police officers. Attach to a tongue depressor and use as stick puppets.)

Firefighter's Hat

Copy onto red construction paper. Cut out the hat.

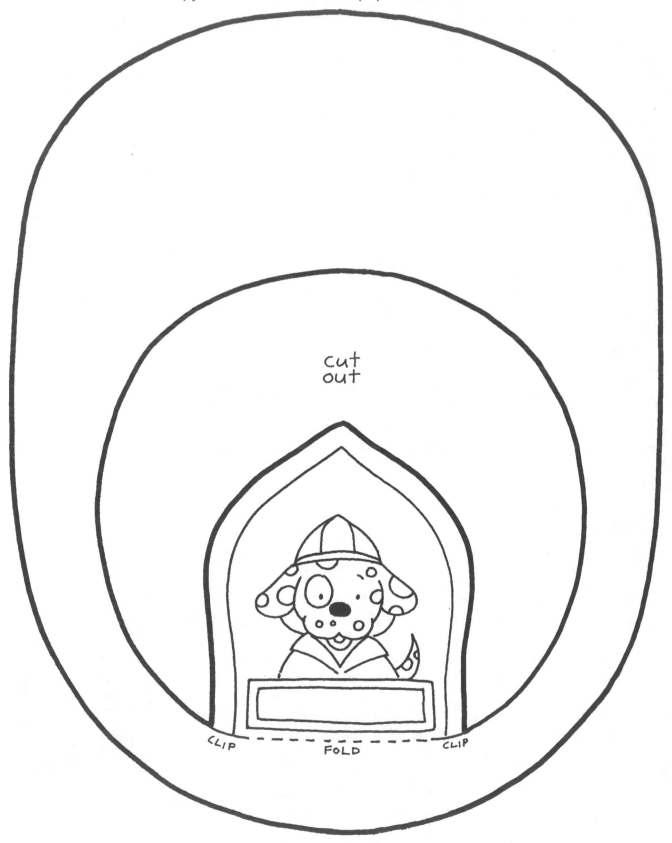

School Bus Pattern

Directions are found on page 32.

Oscar the Grouch's Trash Can

Directions are found on page 32.

Theme 6: Autumn is a Colorful Time (Autumn)

	Activity 1	Activity 2	Activity 3	Activity 4
Monday	**DISCUSSION TOPIC: AUTUMN** This week the children are going to talk about the season called "autumn." In many areas of North America, autumn causes many changes. What are some autumn changes that you notice where you live?	**LEAF PEOPLE** Go on a leaf hunt. Have each child find one large leaf. Glue the leaf to a sheet of paper and then draw arms, legs, and a face.	**BOOKS ABOUT AUTUMN** Bring in a variety of library books about the autumn season. Look through the books together as a class and discuss all the special autumn jobs: raking leaves, harvesting foods, covering flowers, covering windows, and bringing in outside furniture. Pantomime some of the jobs.	**CHANGING COLORS** Talk about how the leaves change colors. Using watercolors or food coloring, demonstrate for the children how you can mix two colors together to create a new color.
Tuesday	**DISCUSSION TOPIC: DIFFERENT CLOTHES FOR DIFFERENT SEASONS** What kinds of clothes do we wear in the summer? What kinds of clothes are we going to need to wear in the autumn? How is the weather changing?	**DRESS FOR THE WEATHER** Complete directions for this activity can be found on page 38.	**LEAF PILES** Leaves are falling, To the ground. Leaves are twirling, All around. Rake the leaves into a pile. Jump in and land, With a smile! Have the children memorize the rhyme.	**NATURE WALK** Take the children on a nature walk. Let them collect things along the way. Talk about all the changes. Look for squirrels. What are the squirrels doing? Are they busy collecting food for the winter? Sort the leaves according to size and color.
Wednesday	**SHOW-AND-TELL WEDNESDAY** **DISCUSSION TOPIC: ANIMALS PREPARING FOR WINTER** Animals experience many changes preparing for winter. Some eat a lot so they can sleep all winter. Many animals store food to eat during the long winter months.	**LITTLE LACING SQUIRREL** The reproducible squirrel pattern and directions can be found on page 39.	**BEARS** Bears are busy eating so they are fat enough to sleep through the winter. Talk about bears and learn the rhyme found on page 40.	**LITTLE BEARS THEY GO TO SLEEP** *(Sung to the tune of "Mary Had a Little Lamb.")* Little bears they go to sleep. Go to sleep. Go to sleep. Little bears they go to sleep. And stay asleep all winter. **MOVEABLE BEAR** Complete directions are found on page 40.
Thursday	**DISCUSSION TOPIC: FOOTBALL** During the summer season people play baseball. Now that it is autumn people like to watch and play football. Have you ever played or watched football? Who has a football they could bring to school so we could try playing the game?	**FALL TREE** Let the children finger paint with the traditional fall colors: red, yellow, orange, and brown. When the painting is dry, cut out leaf shapes. Tape a large brown tree trunk to the wall or bulletin board and add branches. Tape the finger painted leaves to the tree.	**SORTING FALL LEAVES** Sort the leaves according to size and color. Work on the concepts of same and different. Show the children two maple leaves and one oak leaf. Which two are the same? Which one is different? Show the children two red leaves and one brown leaf. Which two are the same? Which one is different?	**FALL TREATS** Children will love warm apple cider served with graham crackers. Graham crackers are a great deal of fun when cream cheese is spread on them. As an extra treat add raisin facial features.
Friday	**SPECIAL NEWS FRIDAY** **DISCUSSION TOPIC: AUTUMN COLORS** What season comes after autumn? What changes do we will see when winter arrives?	**WHAT A COLORFUL TREE** Copy the tree pattern found on page 42 for each child. Provide the children with autumn-colored crayons and let them experiment with adding color to the top of the tree. Encourage the children to draw some animals in their pictures. What animals would they see by a tree?	**LEAF GRAPHING** Use all the leaves that the children have collected and make a graph. Graph according to the shape or color of the leaves.	**LET'S PLAY CONCENTRATION** Use the autumn card patterns found on page 41. Make two sets of each and play concentration. You can also make four identical card sets and play "Go Collect" *(instead of "Go Fish").*

Dress for the Weather

Copy the boy and girl patterns and the clothes.
Color and cut out. Dress them for autumn weather.

Lacing Card Squirrel

Copy the squirrel on brown card stock. Punch holes where indicated. Lace the card.

TEDDY BEAR, TEDDY BEAR

Teddy bear, teddy bear, turn around.
Teddy bear, teddy bear, touch the ground.
Teddy bear, teddy bear, reach up high.

Teddy bear, teddy bear, touch the sky.
Teddy bear, teddy bear, touch your shoe.
Teddy bear, teddy bear, I love you!

(The children should dramatize the rhyme as they say it.)

Moveable Bear

Copy onto brown card stock. Cut out and punch holes where indicated.
Attach arms, legs, and head with brass fasteners.

Autumn Concentration

Directions are found on page 37.

What a Colorful Tree!

Directions are found on page 37.

Theme 7: It's Harvest Time! (Seeds and Harvesting)

	Activity 1	Activity 2	Activity 3	Activity 4
Monday	**DISCUSSION TOPIC: VEGETABLE GARDENS** The children are going to talk about the harvest season of autumn. During autumn, many vegetables have grown enough to be harvested and eaten. Who has a garden at home? Have you begun picking the vegetables? Send a note home asking the parents to send some vegetables to school.	**THE PUMPKIN STORY** Read to the children, *The Story of How a Pumpkin Grows,* found on page 44. This is a reproducible page that the children can bring home to share with their parents.	**SEED PICTURES** Complete directions for making seed pictures can be found on page 45.	**A REAL PUMPKIN** After you have discussed the story of *How a Pumpkin Grows.* Bring in a real pumpkin, cut it open, and let the children touch and feel the seeds. Wash the seeds and toast them for a special treat. The recipe for toasting pumpkin seeds can be found on page 45.
Tuesday	**DISCUSSION TOPIC: VEGETABLES** Ask the children who likes to eat vegetables. Make a graph of all the vegetables that the children like and the ones that they do not like. Where do vegetables come from?	**VEGETABLE COLLAGE** Provide the children with discarded magazines and the grocery section of the newspaper. Have the children find pictures of vegetables. Cut out all the vegetable pictures and glue them on a large sheet of paper.	**VEGETABLE SOUP** Let the children have the fun of making a big pot of vegetable soup. The recipe can be found on page 45.	**VEGETABLE STAND** Arrange on a vegetable stand, the left over "cleaned and chopped" vegetables from the vegetable soup activity. Have the children shop at the vegetable stand with a small paper plate. They can enjoy sampling raw vegetables and compare the tastes with the cooked vegetable soup.
Wednesday	**SHOW-AND-TELL WEDNESDAY** **DISCUSSION TOPIC: SEEDS** Seeds create all the plants and trees. Who knows how seeds travel? Some seeds float through the air. Some seeds are moved by birds and insects. Some seeds just fall to the ground.	**LET'S OBSERVE SEEDS** Bring in a milkweed or cattail to show the children, then guide them into the following discussion: What is a seed for? Why does a plant make a seed? How does a seed get planted? Arrange a table with many kinds of seeds for the children to examine.	**CATTAILS** Take a cattail outside, blow on it and watch the seeds float away. This is a great demonstration. The children will really be able to see how seeds travel through the air.	**LITTLE SEED** Little seed so soft and round, Safely planted in the ground. Watered by the rain And warmed by the sun. A tiny plant will grow– Oh, how much fun!
Thursday	**DISCUSSION TOPIC: HARVEST ACTIVITIES** On Monday the children talked about vegetables and all the things that grow in a garden. Today let's make a graph. At the bottom we will list all the names of the vegetables. Let's see how many people like and dislike the vegetables.	**WEED ARRANGEMENTS** Bring in a large variety of dried weeds. Let the children have the fun of arranging the weeds in paper cups. Place clay or playdough at the bottom of the cup and press the weeds into the clay or playdough.	**BEAN PLANTS** Ask the children to bring in cans or small flower pots. Fill the pots with dirt and plant bean seeds. In 7 to 10 days the plants will sprout. Write daily observations about the planted seeds.	**ACORNS AND LEAVES** Have the children sort acorns and leaves according to size. Patterns are found on page 46.
Friday	**SPECIAL NEWS FRIDAY** **DISCUSSION TOPIC: PICKLE FUN** Pickles are made from cucumbers. Have a fun pickle-tasting party. Pickles come in a wide variety of flavors. Make a graph showing which pickles were the favorites.	**CUCUMBER ANIMALS** Large cucumbers can be made into interesting animals. Add toothpick legs. Glue on eyes, ears, and hair. Name your silly animal.	**REFRIGERATOR PICKLES** This is a wonderful recipe for refrigerator pickles. The complete recipe can be found on page 45.	**PICKLE PRINTS** Cut a cucumber is half. Dip one end in fall-colored paint and print on paper. Let the children make a creative collage of fall colors.

Copy for each child. Have the children color, cut out, and staple in proper sequence.

The Story of How a Pumpkin Grows

The pumpkin seeds are planted in the soil.

The pumpkin seeds need sun and water.

Soon, the seeds begin to sprout and grow.

The leaves turn into vines.

Blossoms begin to grow.

Small green pumpkins grow where the blossoms were growing.

The green pumpkins turn orange as they get bigger.

When it gets cooler outside the pumpkins are ready to be picked.

SEED PICTURES

The children will need construction paper, black markers, glue, and a variety of large seeds. The best seeds for this activity can be found in pumpkins and large squash. Wash and dry the seeds.

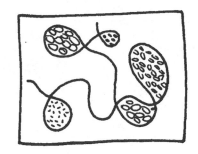

Ask the children to draw a scribble design with the black marker on a piece of construction paper. Fill each section with glue and have the children place the seeds on the glue. The seed designs are attractive and it is a great exercise for developing fine motor skills.

TOASTED PUMPKIN SEED RECIPE

Toasted pumpkin seeds are a great snack that many children will enjoy. They especially enjoy this treat if they have been the ones to actually scoop out the seeds from a real pumpkin.

You will need: Approximately 2 cups of washed pumpkin seeds, 1-1/2 tablespoons melted butter, and 1-1/2 teaspoons of salt.

Directions: Rub oil onto a cookie sheet. In a large bowl mix together the seeds, salt, and butter. Spread the seeds on a cookie sheet and bake in a 250° oven for about 2 hours or until brown and slightly crisp.

VEGETABLE SOUP

This is a fun activity that will take some teacher or parent preparation. Send a note home a few days before you plan to make this soup asking the children to bring in something for the soup.

Before you begin the cooking activity, review the names of all the vegetables with your class. Some good vegetables to include in the soup are peas, carrots, potatoes, celery, corn, and green beans.

You will need: The above vegetables *(chopped and ready to be cooked),* a crock pot or slow cooker, tomato juice, water, salt, and pepper.

Directions: Let the children wash the vegetables. Add them to the crock pot filled with one part tomato juice and one part water. Salt and pepper to taste. Let cook until the vegetables are soft. Serve in small paper cups with plastic spoons.

REFRIGERATOR PICKLES

You will need: 9 cucumbers thinly sliced, 1 sliced onion, 1 cup of chopped green peppers, 2 teaspoons salt, and 1 teaspoon celery seed.

Directions: Mix all the ingredients together and pour over the cucumbers. Add 2 cups sugar and 1 cup vinegar and refrigerate. By the next day the cucumbers should be ready to be eaten.

Acorn and Leaf Patterns
Directions are found on page 43.

Theme 8: Let's Pretend! (Pumpkin Fun)

	Activity 1	Activity 2	Activity 3	Activity 4
Monday	**DISCUSSION TOPIC: OWLS** *To the teacher:* Many schools are choosing not to participate in Halloween activities. This thematic unit could be used as a modified Halloween unit. There are no witches or ghosts. This unit talks about pumpkins, bats, and owls.	**REAL OWLS** Who know what animal says, "whoo-whoo?" That's right—an owl. Let's look at some pictures of real owls. Continue talking about real owls. What have we learned from the books? Owls sleep during the day while they hunt and eat at night.	**FLYING OWL** Complete directions for this activity can be found on page 48.	**WHOO-WHOO** "Whoo-whoo," said the owl, Sitting in the tree. "During the day, I'm quiet as can be." "Whoo-whoo," said the owl, "I'm awake at night." "I hunt, I eat, and then sleep, When it's light."
Tuesday	**WHAT'S REAL AND WHAT'S PRETEND** Whether or not you celebrate Halloween, this is a time of year where children are seeing things that are scary. Talk about things that they may be seeing that are not real, such as displays in stores or commercials on TV.	**THERE'S A MONSTER IN MY CLOSET** Read the book, *There is a Monster in My Closet,* by Mercer Mayer. Children delight in the realization that the monster is really afraid of the child!	**MY CLOSET** Have children draw a picture of a silly monster. Out of brown construction paper cut out a door that is larger than the monster. Tape one side of the door on the paper. Now you can open and close the closet door to see the monster.	**PLAY DRESS UP** A dress up corner is a wonderful creative play area. If you don't already have one in your classroom, encourage parents to donate clothes for this area. Imaginative play is so important in early childhood.
Wednesday	**SHOW-AND-TELL WEDNESDAY** **DISCUSSION TOPIC: BATS** Show children pictures of real bats. Bats are wonderful for keeping the insect populations down. There are many misconceptions about bats. Share all the good things about bats.	**BLACK CONSTRUCTION PAPER BATS** Give each child a 9" x 12" piece of black construction paper. Fold the paper like an accordion fan. Draw a face on a black construction paper circle using white chalk. Glue the face to the center, attach a string, and hang from the ceiling.	**RHYMING WITH BAT** The word bat is a member of the –at family. How many words can the class come up with that rhyme with the word bat?	**THREE LITTLE BATS** Three little bats Hanging upside down. One saw a bug And flew off to town. Two little bats, wake up at night. One saw a firefly, And flew off to the light. Hanging all alone, one little bat. Gobbled up a mosquito, Just like that!
Thursday	**DISCUSSION TOPIC: REAL PUMPKINS** If possible, arrange for a field trip to a pumpkin patch. Children love seeing all the pumpkins growing. If this is not possible, bring a real pumpkin to school and allow the children to assist in "cleaning" out of the pumpkin. This is a wonderful activity for teaching such concepts as "in and out" and "inside and outside." **PUMPKIN SCIENCE** This can also be a great science activity. The reason the jack-o'-lantern has a face is so a candle can burn. Fire needs air and without air the fire will go out. Demonstrate this concept with a votive candle and a jar.		**MATCHING JACK-O'-LANTERN FACES** Make a lotto game with a variety of jack-o'-lantern faces. Make a six-square board with six different faces. Make corresponding cards. Place in a learning center and let the children enjoy matching the identical faces.	**PUMPKIN PUZZLE** Complete directions for the pumpkin puzzle can be found on page 49.
Friday	**SPECIAL NEWS FRIDAY** **OUR OWN PUMPKIN PATCH** Create your own pumpkin patch. Have the children finger paint a light blue sky. Use this to cover the top of a bulletin board. Finger paint the bottom of the bulletin board green.	**PUMPKINS FOR THE PATCH** Give each child a small dessert-size paper plate. Paint the plate orange and add a green stem and leaves. Staple or tape the pumpkins to the bulletin board.	**PUMPKIN PARTY** Instead of a Halloween party, you can have a "Pumpkin Party." Draw faces on orange pumpkins and hang as decorations. Serve an orange drink, carrots and dip, orange jello, and as a special treat "Krispie Pumpkin Treats." Follow the directions on a box of Rice Krispies™ to make rice krispie treats. Mold them into flat pumpkin shapes. The children can frost their own krispie pumpkin treats with orange frosting and add raisins for eyes, a nose, and a mouth.	

Flying Owl

Copy for each child. Color, cut out, and attach the wings with brass fasteners.
This owl can be used with the rhyme "Whoo-Whoo" found on page 47.

Pumpkin Puzzle

Copy, color, cut out, and glue together in the correct sequence.

49

Theme 9: People Move in Many Ways (Transportation)

	Activity 1	Activity 2	Activity 3	Activity 4
Monday	**DISCUSSION TOPIC: TRAFFIC LIGHTS** This week the children are going to talk about "**transportation**." Who knows what the word "transportation" means? It is all the ways that people travel and move on land, on water, and in the air. We should talk about safety before we talk about cars, boats, trains, and planes.	**TRAFFIC LIGHTS** What colors do we see on traffic lights? What do they mean. Here is an easy rhyme to help us remember: **Red on top means Stop, stop, stop! Green below means Go, go, go! Yellow in the center means stop is better.**	**RED LIGHT/GREEN LIGHT** Make three circles (red, yellow, and green) and attach to tongue depressors or paint stir sticks. Let the children pretend they are driving cars. When you hold up a red sign, all driving should stop. When you hold up a green sign the children may drive again. Children should be taught to stop when they see a yellow light.	**CLASSROOM BEHAVIOR TRAFFIC LIGHT** Use large cardboard circles with self-stick Velcro™ so the circles can be changed. A green circle means all is well. A yellow circle means the room is getting too noisy—the children should quiet down. A red circle means quietly go to your seat and sit down.
Tuesday	**DISCUSSION TOPIC: TRAVEL BY LAND** Today the children are going to talk and make a list about all the ways we can **travel on land**. This should be the longest list of the week. Cut out land-vehicle pictures from magazines. Make a road on a bulletin board and display the vehicles. (Ask the children to bring in shoe boxes this week.)	**THE TRAIN** A train is coming Down the track. Clickety, clickety, Clickety-clack! Whenever it goes, The whistle blows. You can hear it Wherever it goes!	**COLOR BY NUMBER TRAIN** Complete directions for this reproducible activity can be found on page 51.	**OUR CLASSROOM TRAIN** The boxes the children brought to school will be the train cars. Have each child paint his or her box and glue white paper windows on the sides. Glue small black circles on the bottom of the box for the wheels. With yarn, attach all the cars to create your classroom train.
Wednesday	**SHOW-AND-TELL WEDNESDAY** **DISCUSSION TOPIC: TRAVEL BY WATER** Today we are going to talk about ways that we can **travel on water**. Let's make another list and find pictures of boats, ships, etc. Create a section of water on the bulletin board and add the water vehicles.	**SAILING** Sailing over the ocean blue. Splashing waves, Fish jumping too! The wind moves us fast, We're home at last. Sailing over the ocean blue.	**FLOATING BOATS** This is a water table activity. Give the children aluminum foil. Ask them to mold the foil into the shape of a boat. Put the boats in the water. Does it float? Can you put things in the boat and does it still float? How many things can your boat hold? Perform the same experiments with clay.	**BOAT AND WATER PICTURES** Draw a picture of a boat with crayons. Press hard with the crayon. Paint over the crayon drawing with light blue water color. The watercolor will resist the crayon and will look like water and sky.
Thursday	**DISCUSSION TOPIC: TRAVEL BY AIR** Today we are going to talk about ways that we can **travel in the air**. Let's make another list and find pictures of airplanes, helicopters, spaceships, rockets, and gliders. Add these pictures to the top (sky) area of the bulletin board.	**AIRPLANES** Teach the children how to make folded airplanes. Go outside and fly the planes.	**PARACHUTES** Parachutes are fun to make and even more fun to play with. Use scarves or handkerchiefs. Tie a string on each corner and then attach a small rock, block, or something small that has some weight to it. Throw the parachute up in the air and then let it float to the ground.	
Friday	**SPECIAL NEWS FRIDAY** **DISCUSSION TOPIC: TRANSPORTATION** Look at our bulletin board with all the land, water, and air vehicles that we have found. Today, let's add some finishing touches: clouds, trees, birds, sun, and people.	**TRANSPORTATION PICTURES** Complete directions and reproducible patterns can be found on pages 52–53.	**TRANSPORTATION BINGO, TIC-TAC-TOE, AND LOTTO** Use the patterns found on pages 52–53 not only as discussion starters and pictures for sorting and categorizing, but also for board games such as tic-tac-toe, bingo, and lotto.	**BY LAND, BY SEA, AND BY AIR MURAL** Complete directions for this reproducible activity page can be found on page 54.

Color by Number Train

Color according to the chart.

Red=1   Blue=2   Yellow=3   Green=4   Purple=5

Transportation Patterns

Additional ideas can be found on page 50.
Copy, color, and glue onto index cards. Display the pictures and ask the following questions.

1. Which one is used for traveling to the moon?
2. Which one is used for children to ride to school?
3. Which one is used for hauling building supplies?
4. Which one could we use in a river?
5. Which one do we park in a garage?
6. Which one would you use to ride to a friend's house?
7. Which one moves by the wind?

8. Which one delivers the mail?
9. Which one travels on the ocean?
10. Which one travels over the ocean?
11. Which one travels on tracks?
12. Which one has wings on the top?
13. Which one floats in the air?
14. Which one helps move big boats?

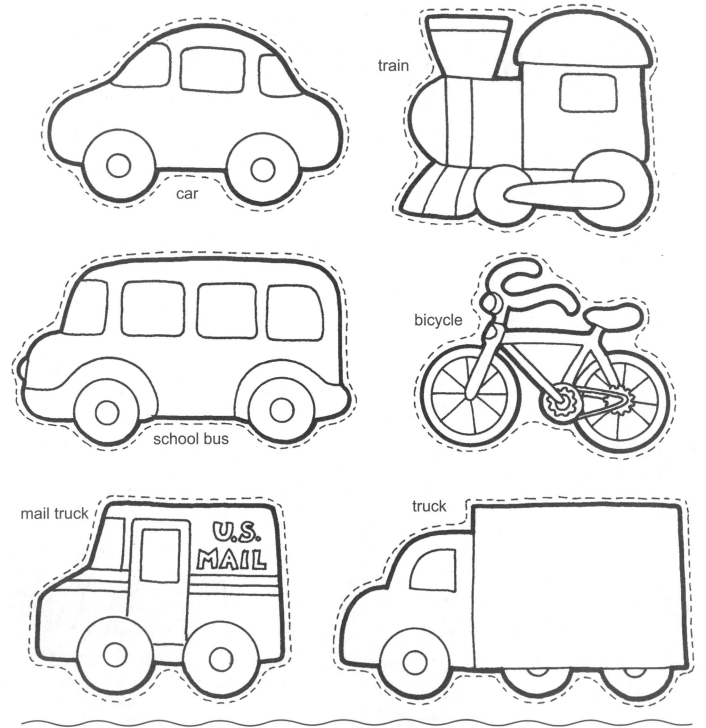

car

train

school bus

bicycle

mail truck

U.S. MAIL

truck

Transportation Patterns Continued . . .

Additional ideas can be found on page 50.

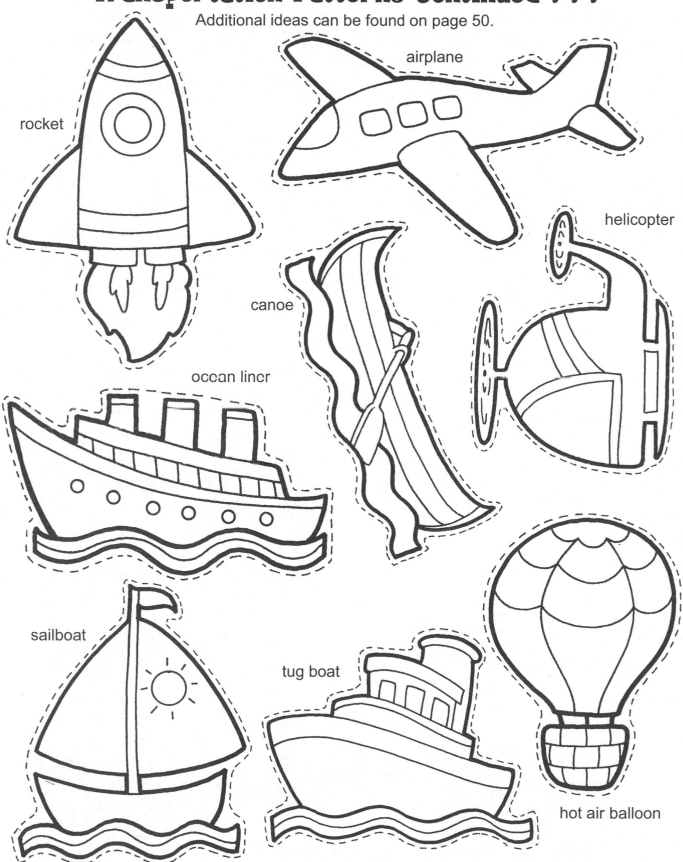

rocket

airplane

helicopter

canoe

ocean liner

sailboat

tug boat

hot air balloon

By Land, By Sea, and By Air!

Directions are found on page 50.

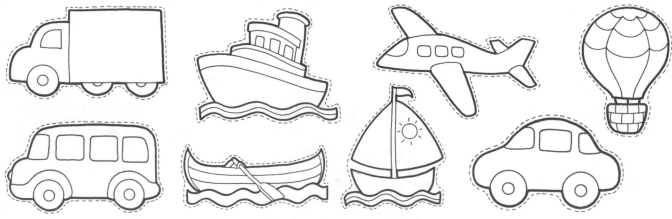

Theme 10: Those Magic Words! (Manners)

	Activity 1	Activity 2	Activity 3	Activity 4
Monday	**DISCUSSION TOPIC: BEING CONSIDERATE AND LOOKING AT THE FEELINGS OF OTHERS** This week the children are going to be talking about "**good manners**" and all the reasons why it is so important to be polite. The main reason that good manners are important is because they help us learn to be "considerate" people. Being considerate simply means that we are thinking about the feelings of others. When people are rude and impolite it can hurt people's feelings. Do you like people who have nice manners and are considerate? How do you feel about people who are rude and inconsiderate?		**LOLLIPOP FACES** Attach two construction paper circles to the top of a tongue depressor or craft stick. On one side of the circle draw a happy face. On the other side of the circle draw a sad face. Give the children many real-life examples of considerate and inconsiderate behavior. The children hold up their lollipops showing a sad or happy face.	**HOW DOES IT MAKE YOU FEEL?** Help the children learn to recognize considerate behavior. Use the reproducible activity sheet found on page 56 as a class project.
Tuesday	**DISCUSSION TOPIC: USING MAGIC WORDS** Ask the children if anyone has ever heard of magic words? If so, what are the magic words? For the purpose of today's lessons, the magic words that are going to be discussed are: **please**, **thank you**, **excuse me**, and **I'm sorry**.	**CATCH YOU BEING GOOD** Create a "Magic Words" bulletin board. Cut out a black construction paper magician's top hat for each child. Print the child's name on the brim. Each time you catch a child using one of the magic words, that child gets to put a sticker on his or her top hat. Send the hats home at the end of the week.	**MAGIC WORD PENNANTS** Let each child design a magic words pennant. The child can take it home and display it on the refrigerator to help him or her remember to use the magic words.	**MANNERS ARE IMPORTANT** Use the reproducible activity found on page 57.
Wednesday	**SHOW-AND-TELL WEDNESDAY** **DISCUSSION TOPIC: THE IMPORTANCE OF SHARING AND CARING** Having good manners also means knowing when to share and how to show people we care about them.	**I LIKE ____, BECAUSE ____!** Use the reproducible activity found on page 56. Seat the children in a group and say, "I like___, because___." Let the children come up with ideas about each other. Write down the responses and put the papers on display. Add one each day so by the end of the week, all the children have several to take home.	**MAKE SOMEONE SMILE** This is a fun game that all children seem to love. Have two children sit face to face and stare at each other and try not to smile. Time the children to discover how long it took until someone smiled. The lesson is: It is more fun to smile and be pleasant. It is hard work to be grouchy.	**LEARNING TO CARE AND SHOW EMPATHY** Here are some role playing activities. 1. Pretend there is a new child at school. What could the children do to make the child's day easier? 2. Mom isn't feeling well today. How can you help her feel better? 3. One of your friends looks sad. What can you do?
Thursday	**DISCUSSION TOPIC: THE IMPORTANCE OF BEING HONEST & TRUSTWORTHY** Discuss the word honesty. What does it mean? Use examples such as: we tell the truth and do not lie; we respect the property of others; and, we do not take things that do not belong to us.	**PINOCCHIO** Read or tell the story of Pinocchio. This puppet has to earn the privilege to become a real boy and has many adventures. One of Pinocchio's biggest lessons is learning not to tell lies. Every time he lies his nose grows! *(Use a puppet as you tell the story.)*	**GEORGE WASHINGTON** Our first president is also famous for being incredibly truthful. It is said that as a child he chopped down the cherry tree in his parents' yard, but said, "I cannot tell a lie. I chopped down the cherry tree." Bring in cherries for the children to sample. Discuss the times that they were honest and truthful with their parents.	**THE LITTLE BOY WHO CRIED WOLF** This is another wonderful story that illustrates the horrible things that can happen when someone tells a lie. Have the children act out the story as you tell it. Let the children draw a picture of a sheep to help them remember the story.
Friday	**SPECIAL NEWS FRIDAY** **PUTTING IT ALL TOGETHER: MANNERS TEA PARTY** Today the children are going to have a tea party. They will use magic words, be considerate and caring of one another, and will use nice table manners.	**TABLE MANNERS** Here are some good rules to review and practice with the children at the tea party. 1. Never reach across the table for food. Ask someone to pass it to you. Remember to say "please" and "thank-you." 2. Do not talk with your mouth full of food. 3. Do not put your elbows on the table. 4. If your food is too hot, wait for it to cool. 5. Do not spit out food that you do not like. Swallow it with a drink of water. 6. Remember to put your napkin on your lap.		**THE TEA PARTY** Serve warm apple cider *(most young children do not like tea)* and cookies. Set the table with placemats and napkins. Discuss table manners as you enjoy the cider and cookies. Before you serve the treats make sure everyone has napkins on their laps and no elbows on the table. Enjoy!

How Does It Make You Feel?

Copy this page for each child. Read the statements to the class. If the statement makes the child feel happy, the child should circle a happy face. If the statement makes the child feel sad, they should circle a frowning face.

1. Call someone a bad name.

2. Helped mom set the table.

3. Teased your little brother.

4. Picked up your toys.

1. Fed the dog.

2. Remembered to brush teeth.

3. Pinched the cat.

4. Said "Thank you" for a gift.

I like. _____

because. _____

_____

Manners Are Important!

Look at each box and decide what each animal is saying.
Cut out the words at the bottom of the page and paste them in the correct scene.

Little kitten spilled the milk!

Bunny wants some more carrots.

Dad bought puppy a new toy.

Little skunk made it stink.

Please

Thank You

I'm Sorry

Excuse me

Theme 11: I Am Grateful! (Thanksgiving)

	Activity 1	Activity 2	Activity 3	Activity 4
Monday	**DISCUSSION TOPIC: THE FIRST THANKSGIVING** This week the children are going to talk about **Thanksgiving**. Ask the children if they know why we celebrate Thanksgiving. Today tell the children about the first Thanksgiving. Read the background on page 59. Provide the children with books and pictures about Thanksgiving.	**A MAYFLOWER JOURNEY** Pretend to take a journey on the Mayflower. What should you bring on the journey? What would it be like not to see land for months and months? What do you think the people did on the boat to pass the time? Pretend to spot land. What do you see when you arrive in America?		**THANKSGIVING PUPPETS** Complete directions for the reproducible activity "Thanksgiving Puppets" are found on page 60.
Tuesday	**DISCUSSION TOPIC: NATIVE AMERICANS** Indian people—the Native Americans—were here in America. They are a great people, who, as we learned about yesterday, taught the Pilgrims how to grow food so they could take care of themselves.	**CORN ON THE COB** The Indian people taught the Pilgrims how to grow corn. Draw an outline of a piece of corn. With a paintbrush, apply glue on the inside of the outline. Use "popcorn" kernels and fill the outline to make a corn on the cob.	**CHIPPEWA BANNOCK** Native American people are known for fried bread. It is delicious and a traditional food. You will need: 2 cups flour, 1/4 teaspoon salt, 1 tablespoon shortening, 1 cup sour milk, 1 teaspoon baking soda in 1/2 cup water. Combine all the ingredients and mix into the flour. Form into a large flat circle. Fry in an electric frying pan.	**COLORFUL TEPEE** Native American people do not live in tepees now, but many once did. The tepees were beautiful and strong. Complete the reproducible activity found on page 61.
Wednesday	**SHOW-AND-TELL WEDNESDAY** **DISCUSSION TOPIC: TURKEYS** Thanksgiving turkeys became a tradition because Native Americans always had fall harvest celebrations. They ate the food they grew and enjoyed eating deer and wild turkeys.	**LITTLE TURKEY** Little turkey With a tail so wide. You had better run and hide. Don't you know, It's Thanksgiving day. Hide! I won't give you away!	**PAPER BAG TURKEYS** Give each child a lunch-size brown paper bag. Color the top half of the bag with bright colors. Open the bag and stuff half full with newspaper. Tie string around the bag. Spread the colors to look like the turkey's feathers. Add a face with black marker.	
Thursday	**DISCUSSION TOPIC: MORE ABOUT TURKEYS** Did you know that the wild turkey was almost the national bird of the United States of America? Benjamin Franklin thought the turkey was so impressive that he wanted the turkey as the national bird instead of the bald eagle.	**WHERE IS THE TURKEY HIDING?** Use a paper turkey cut out. Hide the turkey and have the children search for it. Use positional and directional words to help guide the children in locating the turkey. The child who finds the turkey gets to be the next one to hide it.	**TURKEY HAND TRACING** Trace each child's hand on a piece of paper. Show the children how to color their hands so they look like turkeys.	**CORN BREAD** Make corn bread with the class. Follow the directions found on the package. Explain to the children how the Native Americans had to grind the corn to make flour. Bake and serve with honey. Yum!
Friday	**SPECIAL NEWS FRIDAY** **DISCUSSION TOPIC: BEING THANKFUL** This week the children learned that Thanksgiving is a holiday when people remember to say "thank you." Let's make a class list of some of the things that we are thankful for.	**GRANDPARENTS HOUSE** Many families share Thanksgiving dinner at their grandparents' homes. Ask who is going to see their grandparents this Thanksgiving. What are some things that you can do to be helpful at your grandparents? Have the children color a picture of their grandparents to bring with them on Thanksgiving.	**PLAN A MEAL** Give each child a piece of paper with a plate, knife, fork, and spoon drawn on it. Have the children draw pictures of their favorite meals. Let the children share their pictures and describe their meals to the class.	**GOING TO GRANDMOTHER'S HOUSE** Let's pretend that we are in the car driving to grandmother's house. What do you see? Do we need to stop for gas? Should we sing some songs in the car? What will we do when we get to grandmother's house?

The First Thanksgiving
Color.

THE FIRST THANKSGIVING

There are many myths involved with the historical interpretation of the first Thanksgiving. When teaching young children about this piece of history, we must remember to teach the important "truths" of this event. The first truth is that it was the first harvest feast that the Pilgrims attended. It was not the first harvest feast for the Native Americans. Traditionally, the Native Americans held as many as six celebration feasts a year.

It is recorded that the Pilgrims landed at Plymouth Rock on December 11, 1620, weak and tired from their seven-week journey crossing the ocean. Having arrived in the winter proved to be devastating for them. Their first concern was to build housing, keep warm, and to survive. Many of the Pilgrims became very sick and many died. By the spring, only 46 of the original 102 Pilgrims were alive (*Of Plymouth Plantation,* by William Bradford, original manuscript, 1627).

The Native Americans recognized that the Pilgrims needed help. Squanto, a Native American from the Wampanoag nation, came and lived with the Pilgrims for several months. He taught them how to grow vegetables, build better homes, how to tap maple syrup from the trees, which plants were poisonous, and many more survival skills. The next harvest was bountiful and the Pilgrims were thankful to their new friend, Squanto.

To celebrate their good fortune, the Pilgrims invited Squanto and his family to a celebration feast—which we now call Thanksgiving. To the Pilgrims surprise, the people in Squanto's nation had large families. Squanto brought 90 family members with him to the feast. This celebration lasted for three days. The people ate outside at long tables and played games.

     59

Thanksgiving Puppets

Directions: Copy onto card stock, color, and cut out the patterns. Attach craft sticks to make stick puppets, self-stick Velcro™ to use on the flannel board, or self-stick magnetic strips to use on a magnetic board. Use the puppets for retelling stories and for making up new stories about Thanksgiving.

60

Early Learning Thematic Lesson Plans

Colorful Tepee!

Trace and color.

Theme 12: It's A Colorful World! (Colors)

	Activity 1	Activity 2	Activity 3	Activity 4
Monday	**DISCUSSION TOPIC: RED AND BLUE** This week the children are going to learn about colors. Today, let's talk about **RED** and **BLUE**. If you are wearing blue, stand up. Stand up if you are wearing red. All week long we are going to build a **COLOR CITY** and each of you are going to make a big book of colors.	**COLOR CITY** Using cardboard, cut out a silhouette of a city and set it on a table. The cut out of the city should have 10 buildings—all white. Each day choose two children—each child will color one of the buildings. Begin this project today. Choose one child to color one building **RED** and another child should color one building **BLUE**. Have the children search the room and find small items that are either red or blue. Place the items on the table by the red or blue building.	**COLOR PUZZLE INTERACTIVE BULLETIN BOARD** Puzzle patterns and complete directions for the interactive bulletin board are found on pages 63–65. Each day, add two more reproducible puzzles to the bulletin board. Today add **RED** and **BLUE**.	
Tuesday	**DISCUSSION TOPIC: YELLOW AND GREEN** Add to Color City. Today color one building **YELLOW** and one building **GREEN**. Have the children search the room and find small objects that are yellow and green and place them by the corresponding building.	**"MY OWN COLOR BIG BOOK"** Give each child a paper with the color word written at the top in the appropriate color. Each day have the children add new color pages. The children may either color a picture in the designated color or find and paste appropriate colored pictures.	**COLOR HOP** Place color squares on the floor. Make sure you have several of each color. Call out directions to the children, for example, "Sam, hop to yellow. Juan, hop to green." The children will delight in all the jumping and will quickly learn to recognize all of the colors.	**COLOR PUZZLE INTERACTIVE BULLETIN BOARD CONTINUED. . .** Add **YELLOW** and **GREEN**. Puzzle patterns are found on page 64.
Wednesday	**SHOW-AND-TELL WEDNESDAY** **DISCUSSION TOPIC: ORANGE AND PURPLE** Add to Color City. Today color one building **ORANGE** and one building **PURPLE**. Have the children search the room and find small objects that are orange and purple and place them by the corresponding building.	**MIXING COLORS** Place shaving cream in plastic bags that seal tightly. Add food coloring and watch the colors turn into new colors. Mix red and blue and discover purple. Mix yellow and red to discover orange. Mix blue and yellow to discover green.	**COLOR LINE** Paint wooden clothespins, each one a different color. Have a variety of solid-colored clothing. Let the children play and pin the clothes up on the clotheslines using the proper colored clothespin. **ADD TO "MY OWN COLOR BIG BOOK"** Add purple and orange.	**COLOR PUZZLE INTERACTIVE BULLETIN BOARD CONTINUED. . .** Add **ORANGE** and **PURPLE**. Puzzle patterns are found on page 64.
Thursday	**DISCUSSION TOPIC: PINK AND WHITE** Add to Color City. Today color one building **PINK** and keep one building **WHITE**. Have the children search the room and find small objects that are pink and white and place them by the corresponding building.	**RAINBOW OF COLORS** Complete directions for this reproducible activity can be found on page 66.	**COLORED TIN CANS** Ask parents to donate coffee cans. Paint each can a different color. Provide a wide variety of objects for the children to sort into the can of the same color. **ADD TO "MY OWN COLOR BIG BOOK"** Add pink and white.	**COLOR PUZZLE INTERACTIVE BULLETIN BOARD CONTINUED. . .** Add **PINK** and **WHITE**. Puzzle patterns are found on page 65.
Friday	**SPECIAL NEWS FRIDAY** **DISCUSSION TOPIC: BROWN AND BLACK** Add to Color City. Today color one building **BROWN** and one building **BLACK**. Have the children search the room and find small objects that are brown and black and place them by the corresponding building.	**COLOR PUZZLES** The interactive bulletin board puzzle patterns can also be used as individual color puzzles. The children will enjoy making their own puzzles. Patterns are found on pages 63–65.	**ADD TO "MY OWN COLOR BIG BOOK"** Add brown and black. The color book is now finished. Punch holes and tie with yarn to make a book. The children can bring this home and share with their parents.	**COLOR PUZZLE INTERACTIVE BULLETIN BOARD CONTINUED. . .** Add **BROWN** and **BLACK**. Puzzle patterns are found on page 65.

Color Puzzles

INTERACTIVE BULLETIN BOARD

Enlarge and copy each of the color puzzles. Color and laminate for durability. Place a strip of self-stick Velcro™ on the back of each of the puzzle pieces. Place the top of the puzzle on the bulletin board. Place a piece of self-stick Velcro™ below the top puzzle piece. Let the children stick the corresponding piece on the bulletin board.

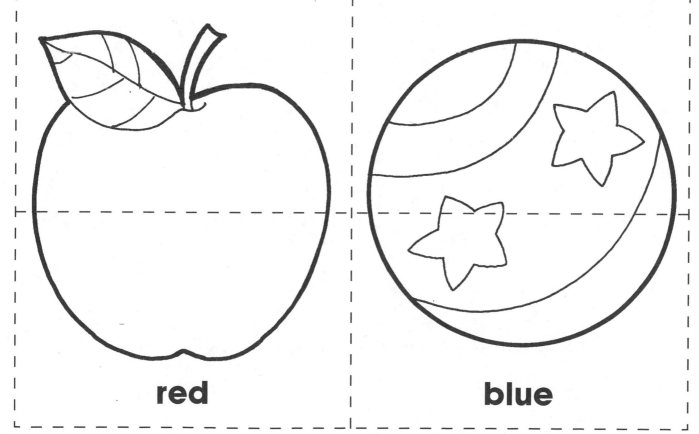

red

blue

Color Puzzles continued . . .

yellow

green

orange

purple

Color Puzzles continued . . .

pink

white

brown

black

Rainbow of Colors!

Color with crayons or watercolor paints.

Theme 13: So Many Holidays! (December Holidays)

	Activity 1	Activity 2	Activity 3	Activity 4
Monday	**DISCUSSION TOPIC: HANUKKAH** This week the children are going to learn about several holidays that are celebrated during the month of December: Hanukkah, Christmas in the United States, Christmas in Australia, Christmas in Mexico, and Kwanzaa. First, we are going to learn about **Hanukkah**.	**HISTORY OF HANUKKAH** Share the history of Hanukkah with the children, found on page 68. **CARDS/WRAPPING PAPER** Blue is a traditional color of Hanukkah. Let the children design blue wrapping paper or greeting cards. Use paint and Hanukkah cookie cutters.	**MENORAH** Using felt, cut out a menorah, eight candles, and eight flames. Place on a flannel board. Have the children add a felt candle and a felt flame for the eight days of Hanukkah. *(A menorah has nine branches—the center candle is used for lighting the others.)*	**CRAFT CANDLES** Make candles from discarded toilet paper tubes. Paint the cardboard tubes and let dry. Add red and orange tissue paper in the top to represent a flame. These candles can be used with the rhyme on page 68. **TRADITIONAL POTATO (LATKE) PANCAKES** The complete recipe can be found on page 68.
Tuesday	**DISCUSSION TOPIC: CHRISTMAS IN MEXICO** Today, the children are going to learn about **Christmas in Mexico**. There are many fun traditions such as Los Posados. *(See page 69 for details.)* "**Feliz Navidad**" means "Merry Christmas" in Spanish. "Feliz Navidad" is a popular recording and a fun song to teach the children.	**REENACT LOS POSADOS** Reenact Los Posados by holding pretend candles and going to other classrooms in the school and asking for shelter. End the procession in your classroom with the fun of breaking a piñata. **EASY PIÑATA** Complete directions are found on page 69.	**THE LEGEND OF THE POINSETTIA** Tell the children "The Legend of the Poinsettia." The legend can be found on page 69, as well as additional poinsettia activities.	**CHOCOLATE** Chocolate is a favorite drink in Mexico. Make chocolate milk in your classroom and learn this verse in Spanish. Children sing this in Mexico. **Uno, dos, tres, cho Uno, dos, tres, co Uno, dos, tres, la Uno, dos, tres, te cho-co-lá-te, cho-co-lá-te.**
Wednesday	**SHOW-AND-TELL WEDNESDAY** **DISCUSSION TOPIC: CHRISTMAS IN AUSTRALIA** Today, the children are going to learn about **Christmas in Australia**. The unusual thing about Christmas in Australia is that it is celebrated in the summertime. Use a globe and explain why to the children.	**REAL TREES** Many people in Australia do not like artificial Christmas trees or chopping down real trees. They will plant a live tree in a pot. The live tree is decorated. What do you think of a real, live Christmas tree? Some people believe it is bad luck to keep the tree in the house longer than 12 days.	**CAROLS BY CANDLELIGHT** This event was begun in 1937 by Norman Banks after he noticed that many people are lonely at Christmas. This event happens in almost every park in Australia. One evening the week before Christmas, everyone can come to the park and sing carols. Sing carols with your class.	**POSTAGE STAMPS** Each year Australia designs special Christmas postage stamps at a reduced rate. Have your class design a Christmas postage stamp. **FATHER CHRISTMAS** Santa Claus is sometimes called Father Christmas in Australia. *(Both wear a red suit.)*
Thursday	**DISCUSSION TOPIC: CHRISTMAS IN THE UNITED STATES** Today the children are going to talk about how people celebrate **Christmas in the United States**. Many families create their own traditions. Encourage the children to share how they celebrate Christmas with their families.	**DEAR SANTA** On page 70 you will find a reproducible journal-writing sheet. Have the children dictate a letter to Santa explaining how well-behaved they have been.	**GIFTS FOR PARENTS** Take pictures of the children using either a Polaroid or digital camera. Tape the picture on a piece of colored construction paper and laminate for durability. Punch a hole in the top and tie a ribbon through the hole. This can be used as a bookmark or Christmas decoration. All parents love photos of their children!	**DECORATE COOKIES** Bring in sugar cookies. Provide the children with a variety of decorating materials: frosting *(in several colors)*, raisins, sprinkles, and small candies. The children will love making special Christmas cookies.
Friday	**SPECIAL NEWS FRIDAY** **DISCUSSION TOPIC: KWANZAA** Today the children are going to learn about Kwanzaa. Kwanzaa is not a religious holiday. It is an African American celebration that takes place in the month of December. Read page 71 to learn more about Kwanzaa.	**KINARA** The candelabra that holds the seven Kwanzaa candles is called a kinara. Make or bring one in and place the candles in the correct order. Learn more about the kinara and Kwanzaa on page 71. Use the illustration as a guide for a kinara art project.	**KARAMU** Karamu is the feast on December 31. One of the purposes of the feast is to remember ancestors. Have the children draw pictures of their grandparents. Talk about things they may have learned from a grandparent.	**EXPLORE CHILDREN'S LITERATURE** There are many wonderful children's books about Kwanzaa. Use the Children's Literature Reference Guide on pages 158–160 for a listing of Kwanzaa books for children.

Hanukkah

THE HISTORY OF HANUKKAH

Hanukkah is a Jewish holiday that is also known as "The Festival of Lights." This is a happy celebration when the Jewish people remember a special night when a miracle happened. Many, many years ago, a foreign king and his army wanted to take over Israel and the temple that was there. The Jewish people fought this King for over three years. They won because of a miracle. The only type of lighting in the temple was created by burning oil in lamps. When the people ran out of oil there would be no more light. When the battle was nearing its end, the people in the temple had only enough oil to give them light for one more day. But then, the miracle of the light happened. Instead of burning for only one day, the oil kept burning for eight days! These extra days gave the Jewish people enough time to prepare more oil and win the battle.

During Hanukkah, we remember the great miracle of light. A candle is lit every night for the eight days of Hanukkah. The candles are displayed in a candle holder called a menorah. The candle on the far right side of the Menorah is lit first. A candle is added from right to left each night. Special foods are also served.

THE EIGHT CANDLES

On the first night, we light candle one.
Children are excited, Hanukkah has begun.
The second night we light candles one and two.
It's fun for me and fun for you.
The third night, we light candles
    one through three.
The light is getting brighter as you can see.
The fourth night, we light all four.
The light shines through the windows and door.

The fifth night, we light candles one through five.
And are so glad that we are alive.
The sixth night, we light all six.
Say a prayer, then have latkes to mix.
The seventh night,
    all seven candles shine bright.
And reminds us there is only one more night.
And finally, we get to light all eight.
Isn't it beautiful! Hanukkah's great!

POTATO PANCAKES (LATKES)

Potato pancakes, or latkes, are a traditional Hanukkah food. Latkes are served as a reminder of how the food was quickly prepared for the Maccabees as they went into battle. The pancakes are fried in oil as a reminder of the miracle of the burning oil.

You will need: 2 pounds of potatoes, 1 onion, 1/2 cup chopped scallions *(including the greens),* 1 beaten egg, salt and pepper to taste, vegetable oil for frying.

Directions: Peel the potatoes and onion. Use a grater for the potatoes and onion. Place in a mesh strainer and press out all the excess liquid into a bowl *(you will use the potato starch that settles to the bottom of the bowl later).* Mix the potatoes, onion, and the starch that is at the bottom of the bowl *(pour off excess liquid).* Add the scallions, egg, and salt. Heat a frying pan and add a small amount of vegetable oil. Press the potato mixture into thin pancake shapes. Place in the pan and fry until golden brown on each side.

Special Hint: You can make these ahead of time at home and freeze them. The potato pancakes can be reheated in a 350° oven.

Kwanzaa

LET'S LEARN ABOUT KWANZAA

Kwanzaa was developed from elements of the African heritage and from the ceremony of appreciation for the "first fruits of the harvest." The elements that made up the original meaning of Kwanzaa were based on the African values of family, community responsibility, commerce, and self-improvement. Kwanzaa was created by Dr. Maulana Karenga in 1966. Today, more than 18 million people celebrate Kwanzaa.

Kwanzaa is built on the seven principles that are known as "Nguzo Saba." Kwanzaa is celebrated for seven days (December 26 through January 1). Each day is dedicated to one of the seven principles and a candle is lit each day representing that principle.

Day 1 – Unity (Umoja/**OO-MO-JAH**)
Stresses the importance of family and the community. *(Light middle black candle.)*

Day 2 – Self-Determination (Kujichagulia/**KOO-GEE-CHA-GOO-LEE-YAH**)
Stresses that we define our interests and make decisions that are the best for the family and community. *(Light innermost red candle.)*

Day 3 – Collective Work and Responsibility (Ujima/**OO-GEE-MAH**)
Stresses that we have obligations to the past, present, and future, and we have a role to play in the community, society, and the world. *(Light innermost green candle.)*

Day 4 – Cooperative Economics (Ujamaa/**OO-JAH-MAA**)
Stresses our collective economic strength and encourages us to meet common needs through mutual support. *(Light middle red candle.)*

Day 5 – Purpose (Nia/**NEE-YAH**)
Stresses that we should set personal goals that benefit the community. *(Light middle green candle.)*

Day 6 – Creativity (Kuumba/**KOO-OOM-BAH**)
Stresses that our creative energy should be used to build and maintain a strong community. *(Light outermost red candle.)*

Day 7 – Faith (Imani/**EE-MAH-NEE**)
Stresses that faith helps us to focus on honoring the best of our traditions, draws upon the best in ourselves, and helps us strive for a higher level of life for all. *(Light outermost green candle.)*

THIS IS A KINARA

The candelabra that holds the seven Kwanzaa candles is called a **kinara**. Make or bring one in and have the children place the candles in the correct order. The kinara should sit on a straw mat (**mkeka**). Ears of corn are on the mat, one to represent each child in the home. A fruit basket (**mazao**) and unity cup (**kikombe cha umoja**) are also on the mat. Children may also wish to color a kinara. Enlarge the illustration next to this activity as a guide to create a reproducible kinara for the children.

Theme 14: It's Cold Out There! (Winter)

	Activity 1	Activity 2	Activity 3	Activity 4
Monday	This week the children are going to talk about **winter**. **DISCUSSION TOPIC: SNOW** Today we are going to learn about **snow**. If you live in a warm climate many of the activities will be new and exciting for the children. Snow falls softly to the ground. Have the children move the way they think snow would fall to the ground.	**SNOW EXPERIMENTS** (1) Bring some snow into the classroom or get ice crystals from inside a freezer. Look at them under a magnifying glass. How many points does a snowflake have? (2) Melt snow and ice in a pan. Will they both turn into water? What is a snowflake? What is ice?	**CLASSROOM SNOW** Bring in a pan of snow or fill the water table with snow. This is especially fun if you live in a warm climate. *(Snow can be made from an inexpensive snow cone machine.)* Let the children dig in the snow, make tiny snowmen, make small igloos, and use kitchen utensils and cookie cutters with the snow.	**LET'S MAKE ICICLES** Give each child a dark blue or black piece of paper. With a paintbrush, brush a thick line of white tempera paint along the top of the paper. Hold the paper upright and blow down, so that the paint drips. This will look like an icicle when dry. For extra fun, sprinkle sugar on the paint before it dries, so it will sparkle.
Tuesday	**DISCUSSION TOPIC: SNOWPEOPLE** Today the children are going to talk about snowmen. How many of you have ever built a snowman? Have any of you ever built snowladies? Who can explain how to build a snowman?	**THREE SNOWMEN** Three big snowmen, Standing in a row. Out came the sun, And one melted so slow. Two big snowmen, Standing up tall. The sun kept shining, Now one is small. One big snowman, He'll be fine, we're told. The wind outside is very cold.	**DOUGH SNOWPEOPLE** Make snowmen with a commercially manufactured light-weight "white" modeling compound that air dries and can be painted, or use this homemade playdough recipe: 1 cup salt; 2 cups flour; 6 teaspoons alum; 2 tablespoons vegetable oil; and 1 cup water. Mix together.	**MARSHMALLOW SNOWPEOPLE** Use a small amount of white glue and glue two or three large marshmallows together. Use scrap fabric for a scarf; toothpick arms; and draw on a face with fine-lined magic markers.
Wednesday	**SHOW-AND-TELL WEDNESDAY** **DISCUSSION TOPIC: LIVING IN THE COLD** What do you think it would be like to live in the snow? Use a large map and talk about all the places in the world where it is cold. Why is it cold there? What are some things that you would need to live in the snow?	**FOLLOW THE SNOW** If you are fortunate enough to live in the snow—this activity is best done outside. Make footprints in the snow and pretend that you are tracking your way back home. If you do not have any snow, make paper footprints and place them around the playground or classroom and pretend the same adventure.	**DOG SLEDS** Complete directions for this activity can be found on page 73. **ESKIMO PEOPLE** Complete directions for this activity are found on page 73.	**SNOW TUNNELS** Children love to crawl! You can provide a great crawling experience when you are talking about the cold and winter. Connect all sorts of large boxes—just like a great big tunnel. Let the children pretend that they are crawling through snow tunnels.
Thursday	**DISCUSSION TOPIC: COLD WEATHER ANIMALS** Some animals like warm weather and some animals like cold weather. Let's make a chart of all the animals that you think like cold weather.	**ANIMAL BULLETIN BOARD** Cover a bulletin board with white paper or cotton batting *(snow)* on the bottom, and on top, a light blue sky with clouds. Enlarge the animal patterns on page 74. Let the children color the animals and add them to the bulletin board. Include a water area for the animals that live in the water.	**ANIMAL TRACKS IN THE SNOW** Complete story and directions are found on page 75.	**MY BROWN BEAR** Each child will need a grocery bag. Draw a bear shape on the bag and cut it out so that there are two identical bear cut outs. Staple along the sides, but leave the top of the head open. Draw a face and then stuff the inside of the bag with newspaper or tissue paper. Staple the head shut.
Friday	**SPECIAL NEWS FRIDAY** **DISCUSSION TOPIC: PLAYING IN THE SNOW** Playing in the snow is a lot of fun. What do you need to wear when you play outside? Discuss proper clothing for the different seasons.	**MITTENS** Give each child two paper mitten cut outs. Attach the two with a string. Let the children create their own design. Tell them the mittens must match. Be careful to draw the same thing on each mitten. Read *The Mitten* by Jan Brett.	**PRACTICE SELF-HELP SKILLS** Ideas to increase fine motor skills can be found on page 73.	**MITTEN MATCH** Complete directions for this reproducible activity can be found on page 76.

DOG SLEDS

In some parts of Alaska and Canada, dogs are trained to pull sleds through the snow. Many different kinds of dogs are trained to do this, but the two best breeds are the Siberian Husky and the Alaskan Malamute. Find pictures of these dogs in the encyclopedia or on the Internet to show the children. How do these two breeds of dogs look the same and how do they look different? Why do they have curled tails?

ESKIMO PEOPLE

Some of the people who have lived in Alaska and northern Canada are called Eskimos. They are good people who do not like to argue or fight. Traditionally, if they have a disagreement they will settle the dispute by arranging a contest. The winner of the contest is then the winner of the argument. Do you think this is a good way to settle an argument? What are some things we could do in our classroom to settle disputes in a peaceful way? Let's make a list of all our good ideas.

SELF-HELP SKILLS

If you are teaching in a cold and snowy area you know how important it is that children learn to properly dress themselves. Getting ready to go outside to play can take a long time if the children in your room need a great deal of help. Here are some ideas to help:

1. Make an incentive chart for each child in your class. Whenever they get ready to go out all by themselves (boots on, coat zipped, hood tied or buttoned), they can put a star on their chart. You would be surprised with how fast children get ready with an incentive.

2. For young children, buttoning, zipping, lacing, tying, and snapping are difficult skills that take time, practice, and patience to master. Provide activities that assist children in developing these skills. Have a "handy" parent make the following wooden boards for your classroom: a board with laces for tying, a board with a zipper, a board with snaps, a board with nuts and bolts, a board with latches, and a board with a key and lock. The possibilities are endless. Children love experimenting with these boards and they strengthen fine motor skills.

3. Pinching clothespins onto a bucket or clothesline, snipping the edges of paper with scissors, playing with pegboards, and playing with modeling clay are also ways to help develop fine motor skills.

Cold Weather Animal Patterns

Use with several activities found on page 72.

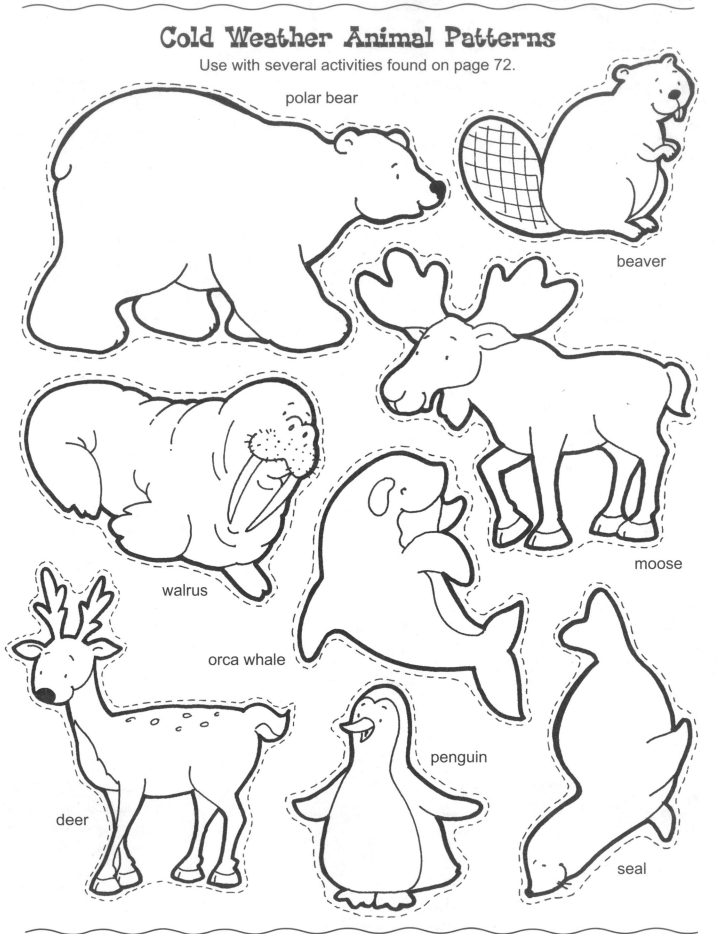

polar bear

beaver

walrus

moose

orca whale

deer

penguin

seal

 Early Learning Thematic Lesson Plans

Animal Tracks in the Snow

This is a story about an Eskimo family. Before we hear the story we should learn a little about the Eskimo people. The people who live along the coastline from the Bering Sea to Greenland, Alaska and northern Canada were once called "Eskimos," but are now called "Inuit," which means "people." *(Show the children this area on a map.)* Many people believe that the Eskimo people lived in igloos. Eskimo people would build igloos or snow huts when they went hunting in the winter. Their homes were traditionally tents. In the summer, the tents were made from caribou or seal skins, and in the winter the shelters were made from sod, stone, or driftwood. They spent a lot of time fishing. Instead of using canoes, the Inuit people made kayaks.

It is winter. Two young Inuit children, Akna *(ahk Na)* and Adlet *(ad LET)*, are going to catch some fish for dinner. They grab their fishing poles and kayak and begin their walk to the water.

As they walk through the snow, they see tracks of animals. To make the walk more fun, they decide to play a guessing game with the animal tracks.

"Look," says Akna. "I see animal tracks that look like a hoof."

"The tracks have wide spaces between them, as if the animal was running," says Adlet.

"I know what animal belongs to those tracks," says Akna. "Those tracks belong to a deer."

The children keep walking. Soon they spot more tracks. "Oh Adlet, look! I see some very small tracks and they disappear at the bottom of that tree," said Akna.

"Look at the top of the tree, Akna. There is a squirrel. Those tracks must belong to the squirrel," Adlet exclaimed.

The children have already seen two types of animal tracks, and there are more to come. Soon, many small tracks were discovered. The tracks look as if a small animal has been hopping in circles. Both the children begin laughing as they see a white rabbit hopping all around in the snow.

When the children are farther away from home, they see some tracks that make them a little nervous. The tracks head toward a small hole hidden below some fallen tree trunks. Before the children can move, a gray fox jumps out from behind the logs and runs off into the woods. The children sigh and are glad that it was a fox, and not a wolf.

The children reach the water, catch some salmon for dinner, and go home. At dinner, as they eat their fish, the children tell their parents about the animal track game they played. That night, they try to draw pictures of the tracks so they would remember what they saw.

(Below are pictures of the animal tracks. Enlarge and copy. Place around the room and let the children discover the tracks as you read the story.)

hind squirrel paw

front squirrel paw

deer hoof

fox paw

rabbit front paw

rabbit back paw

Mitten Match!

Directions: Copy and color two identical mitten boards. Leave one as the playing board and cut the other board into the cards. Place in a learning center and let the children match the mittens!

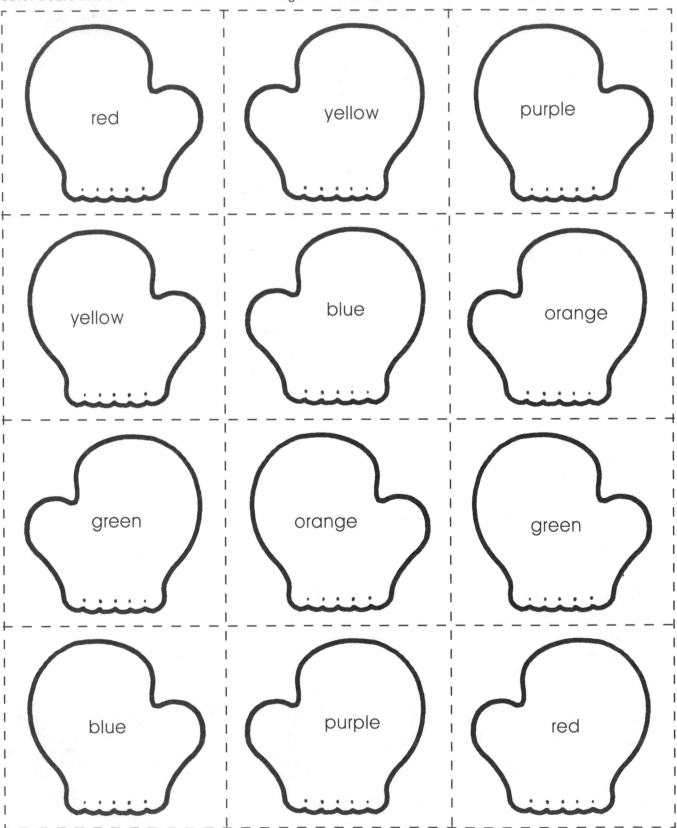

Theme 15: I Am Healthy (Nutrition and Health)

	Activity 1	Activity 2	Activity 3	Activity 4
Monday	**DISCUSSION TOPIC: TEETH** This week the children are going to talk about all the things they need to do to be healthy. The first thing they are going to talk about is their **teeth**. How many teeth do we have? Let's try counting them. Did you know that having a clean, healthy mouth helps your whole body stay healthy?	**WHAT DO WE KNOW?** What do you know about teeth? Why should we brush them? Here is a tune to help you remember: *(Sung to, "Row Your Boat")* Brush, brush, Brush your teeth. Brush two times a day. Brushing, flossing, cleaning, And dental checks, Keeps decay away!	**DECAY EXPERIMENT** Poke a pin hole in the top and bottom of an egg and blow the egg out of the shell. Put the shell in a glass of sugar soda. Ask the children to predict what will happen to the egg shell. Tomorrow check the shell. *(It will be soft.)* Discuss the results. What happens to our teeth when we eat too much sugar?	**HAPPY SMILES** Give each child a yellow circle. Have them draw smile faces on their circles. Provide the children with white squares *(teeth)* and have them give their smile faces huge smiles, with great big white teeth! **CHILDREN'S LITERATURE** Read *Dr. DeSota* by William Steig.
Tuesday	**DISCUSSION TOPIC: HEALTHY EATING** Yesterday the children learned all about teeth. Today they are going to talk about good **food**. It is very important to eat enough of the right foods so our bodies get all the vitamins and minerals they need to stay healthy. When we talk about eating the right food, we are talking about **good nutrition**.	**THE FOOD GUIDE PYRAMID** Provide each of the children with the reproducible *Food Guide Pyramid* found on page 78. Talk about it with the children and have them bring it home to share with their parents. Make a graph of all the children's favorite foods.	**BUILD A CLASSROOM FOOD PYRAMID** On a bulletin board or wall, use masking tape and create the outline of the pyramid. Let the children go through old magazines and newspapers and cut out pictures of food. Tape them to the food pyramid in their proper locations.	**HEALTHY SNACKS** Make special healthy treats with the children and discuss the food groups that are in the following snack. In small paper cups place a couple of spoonfuls of vanilla yogurt (milk). Add berries (fruit - clean and cut into small pieces) and top with granola (grain). Mix and enjoy! Delicious!
Wednesday	SHOW-AND-TELL WEDNESDAY **DISCUSSION TOPIC: DOCTORS** The children have talked about healthy eating and keeping our teeth healthy. Today they are going to talk about seeing the doctor for check-ups to keep their bodies healthy. *(If possible, arrange a field trip to a children's hospital.)*	**DOCTOR SAYS** It is important to be able to name all of our body parts. If we are hurt, we can tell someone what part of our body is hurting. Let's practice by playing, "Doctor Says." This is played just like "Simon Says," only saying "Doctor says, touch your *name a body part*." Only touch if the "Doctor says."	**HOSPITAL OR MEDICAL CLINIC CREATIVE PLAY** A hospital or medical clinic creative play corner is a fabulous addition to any early childhood program. Children can actually overcome many fears about medical experiences when they are allowed to feel in control and "play through" the experiences. All hospital or medical clinic play areas need: an examination room with bandages, stethoscopes, doctor coats, empty bottles for cleaning pretend wounds, cotton balls, pretend syringes, pretend finger pick equipment, paper and pencil to record notes, doll beds, patients *(stuffed animals & dolls)*, paper cups for water or juice, and kitchen equipment for meals. Doll strollers also make good wheelchairs.	
Thursday	**DISCUSSION TOPIC: REST AND EXERCISE** The children are learning so much about being healthy. They have learned about the importance of taking care of their teeth, the importance of eating well, and the importance of seeing a doctor. Today they are going to learn about how they need **rest and exercise** to help their bodies stay healthy.	**REST TIME** First let's talk about why, when we are little, we need to take naps, and why we need to get enough sleep at night. How do you behave when you are tired? How do you feel when you have not had enough sleep? Our bodies get worn out! What helps you go to sleep at night? Read the children a "sleepy" bedtime story.	**WHY EXERCISE?** Why do we need to exercise? What do you think happens to bodies that do not get enough exercise? Exercise every morning to a 1950s rock 'n roll song. Lead the children every morning with jumping jacks, toe touches, arm and leg stretches, and sit ups. The children will love it and it will be good for you, too!	**MY GOOD HEALTH CHART** Copy and send home with the children the reproducible page, *My Good Health Chart*, found on page 79. Include a note encouraging the parents to put it on their refrigerators and add stickers for all the good things the children are doing. This may help with any eating and bedtime problems!
Friday	SPECIAL NEWS FRIDAY **DISCUSSION TOPIC: I AM HEALTHY** Review with the children the previous lessons. Today they are going to talk about being clean. When people look their best—they feel their best. Talk about the importance of bathing, washing hair, and clean clothes.	**PICTURES** Show the children pictures of people who are clean and people who are dirty. Make up silly stories about how they got dirty.	**MAKE BUBBLES** You will need a 1/2 cup liquid dishwashing detergent, 1-1/2 cups warm water, 2 teaspoons sugar, and 1 teaspoon glycerin *(found at any drug store)*. Mix the ingredients together gently and store in a plastic bag that seals tightly. Make blowers for the children out of wire.	**MY GOOD HEALTH BOOK** Copy, cut out, and staple together as a book for each child the reproducible mini-book, *My Good Health Book*, found on pages 80–81. Encourage the children to share these books with their parents.

Food Guide Pyramid

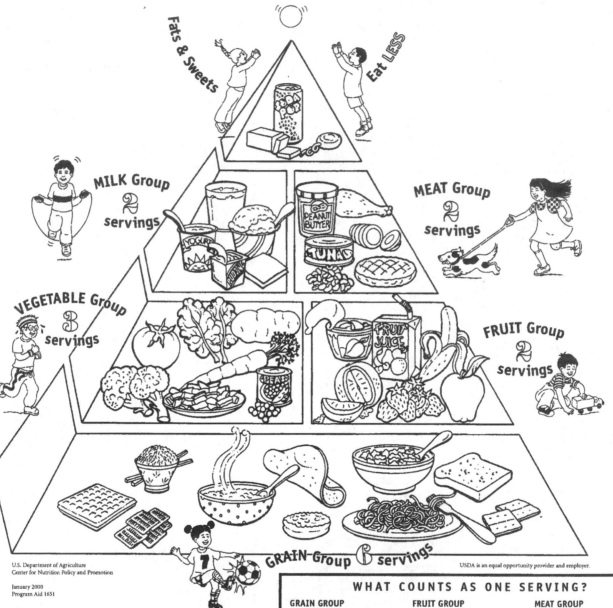

Fats & Sweets

Eat LESS

MILK Group 2 servings

MEAT Group 2 servings

VEGETABLE Group 3 servings

FRUIT Group 2 servings

GRAIN Group 6 servings

PEANUT BUTTER

YOGURT

TUNA

FRUIT JUICE

U.S. Department of Agriculture
Center for Nutrition Policy and Promotion

January 2000
Program Aid 1651

USDA is an equal opportunity provider and employer.

FOOD IS FUN and learning about food is fun, too. Eating foods from the Food Guide Pyramid and being physically active will help you grow healthy and strong.

WHAT COUNTS AS ONE SERVING?

GRAIN GROUP
1 slice of bread
½ cup of cooked rice or pasta
½ cup of cooked cereal
1 ounce of ready-to-eat cereal

VEGETABLE GROUP
½ cup of chopped raw or cooked vegetables
1 cup of raw leafy vegetables

FRUIT GROUP
1 piece of fruit or melon wedge
¾ cup of juice
½ cup of canned fruit
¼ cup of dried fruit

MILK GROUP
1 cup of milk or yogurt
2 ounces of cheese

MEAT GROUP
2 to 3 ounces of cooked lean meat, poultry, or fish.

½ cup of cooked dry beans, or 1 egg counts as 1 ounce of lean meat. 2 tablespoons of peanut butter count as 1 ounce of meat.

FATS AND SWEETS
Limit calories from these.

Four- to 6-year-olds can eat these serving sizes. Offer 2- to 3-year-olds less, except for milk. Two- to 6-year-old children need a total of 2 servings from the milk group each day.

Good Health Chart

Child's name _____

Add a sticker or draw a smile face each time your child completes one of the "good health" tasks.	S	M	T	W	T	F	S
I brushed my teeth in the morning.							
I brushed my teeth in the evening.							
I combed my hair.							
I ate a good breakfast.							
I ate a good lunch.							
I ate a good dinner.							
I took a bath.							
I washed my hands.							
I had a good night's sleep.							
I played and exercised.							

Copy, cut apart, and staple in numerical order. The children may color the pages.

-1-

My Good Health Book

-2-

Remember to brush your teeth twice a day and to visit the dentist.

-3-

Remember to use a tissue and cover your mouth when you sneeze.

-4-

Remember to wash your hands after using the bathroom.

Copy, cut apart, and staple in numerical order. The children may color the pages.

-5-

Remember to get a good
night's sleep every night.

-6-

Remember to
get exercise everyday.

-7-

Remember to eat
foods every day from
all the food groups.

-8-

Remember to take a bath,
wash your hair,
and wear clean clothes.

Theme 16: I Care About You! (Valentine's Day)

	Activity 1	Activity 2	Activity 3	Activity 4
Monday	**DISCUSSION TOPIC: FRIENDSHIP** The theme this week is called "I care about you." The children are going to talk about friendship, people we care about, and celebrating Valentine's Day. Talk about being **friends**. What makes a good friend? What do you do that makes you a good friend?	**SPECIAL FRIENDS GAME** Prepare a heart puzzle for the class. Cut out construction paper hearts. Cut each of the hearts in half. Make sure each heart is different. Pass out the heart-halves to the children and have them walk around the room to find who has the matching half-heart. Once the children find their "matches," they can sit by each other.	**FRIENDSHIP NECKLACES** Provide each child with a 36" piece of string. Wrap masking tape around one end for a needle. Give the children circle shaped cereal, candy, and macaroni. Then have them string a necklace. Next ask the children to give their necklaces away to a friend. Make sure that each child gives and receives a necklace.	**MAILBOX NICE NOTES** Ask each child to bring in a shoebox to decorate as a mailbox. Use them for Valentine's Day and for nice daily notes. Have the children dictate "nice notes" to each other and "mail" them by placing them in the mailboxes. The children can also send pictures. Teachers should write nice notes too!
Tuesday	**DISCUSSION TOPIC: CARING ABOUT FAMILIES** Yesterday the children talked about the importance of being a good friend. Today the children will discuss the **special people in their families**. Who are some of your special family members? Why are these people special to you? What are some nice things that you could do for these people?	**SIX LITTLE VALENTINES** Complete directions and reproducible patterns for *Six Little Valentines* can be found on page 83.	**OLD VALENTINE CARD COLLECTION** Ask parents to send old greeting cards to school. Let the children use these old cards to create new masterpieces to give to some of the special people at school: janitor, cook, and the school secretary.	**A GOOD DEED** Today ask the children to think of a good deed that they could do for someone else. For example: clear the dinner table, feed the cat, pick up toys. The teacher should record the children's responses. Remind them before they go home, and check with them in the morning to see if they followed through with performing their good deed.
Wednesday	**SHOW-AND-TELL DAY WEDNESDAY** Today is **Caring Game Day**. Today the children will learn games that remind them to be good friends and care about each other. Remember to ask who accomplished their good deed.	**BEAN BAG TOSS** Prepare a bean bag board (foam board works well). Cut 4 to 5 holes and write a silly instruction above each hole. For example: "Say something nice to someone wearing green, or give someone a hug who has short hair." The children will giggle a lot while they work on increasing their eye-hand coordination.	**I LIKE YOU** *(Sung to the tune of "London Bridge.")* Did you know that, I like you? I like you. I like you. Did you know that, I like you? I like you. I like you. Let's be good friends. Hold hands and skip in a circle while singing this song.	**FRIENDS GO MARCHING** *(Sung to the tune of, "The Ants Go Marching.")* Friends go marching 1 by 1. Hoorah, hooray! Friends go marching 1 by 1. Hoorah, hooray! Friends go marching 1 by 1. One friend stopped and grabbed *(child's name)* And the 2 have fun, Marching all over the room. *(Continue with 2, 3, and so on, until all the children are marching.)*
Thursday	**DISCUSSION TOPIC: PREPARING FOR VALENTINE'S DAY** It is time to begin preparing for Valentine's Day. Make sure that you have sent notes home to remind parents to send valentines to school. Always keep an extra pack or two on hand for those children who may forget or are not able to bring any.	**THE VERY SPECIAL VALENTINE** Read the book, *The Very Special Valentine,* by Maggie Kneen and Christine Tagg. Talk about what makes a valentine special.	**"I LOVE YOU" LOTTO** Complete directions and reproducible patterns for *I Love You Lotto* can be found on page 84.	**VALENTINE'S DAY CLASSROOM WREATH** Cut out many paper hearts. Have the children work together and glue them on a large cardboard circle. Add a bow at the top. This makes a wonderful Valentine's Day decoration to hang on your door or window.
Friday	**SPECIAL NEWS FRIDAY** **DISCUSSION TOPIC: VALENTINE'S DAY** Happy Valentine's Day! The children have a lot to do to get ready for our party.	**JELLO™ FUN** Jello™ is always a favorite treat of young children. Make red Jello™ according to the directions on the package. Pour into individual clear plastic cups. Top with whipped cream for extra fun!	**SUGAR COOKIE HEARTS** Purchase a box of sugar cookies. Let the children decorate the cookies with pink frosting and sprinkles. Be sure to recruit some parental help for the party!	**PARTY TIME** At the party serve the Jello™, cookies, and pink lemonade. Play musical chairs with music about love and friendship. Read a special valentine story. End the party by letting the children enjoy opening all their valentines.

Six Little Valentines

SIX LITTLE VALENTINES

Six little valentines sitting two by two.
The first valentine says, "I really love you."
The second valentine says, "You have won my heart."
The third valentine says, "Let's never part."

The fourth valentine says, "Do you love me, too?"
The fifth valentine says, "I most certainly do."
The sixth valentine says, "Get ready, it's time!"
We are here to say, "Happy Valentine's!"

(Copy, color, and cut out the six valentine patterns. Let the children hold up the valentines as you say the rhyme. The patterns may also be used for making classroom valentines.)

83

"I Love You" Lotto

Directions: Copy at least six lotto boards and an equal number of sets of cards onto red or pink card stock. Shuffle all the cards and put them face down in a pile. The players take turns drawing cards. A matching card is placed on the board. If the player already has the card, that card must be returned to the bottom of the pile. The first player to cover all eight squares is the winner. Look for the "play again" and "lose a turn" cards!

Theme 17: The Shapes of Things (Shapes)

	Activity 1	Activity 2	Activity 3	Activity 4
Monday	**DISCUSSION TOPIC: CIRCLES & SQUARES** This week the children are going to explore shapes. Can anyone tell us the names of some shapes? Let's talk about **circles** and **squares**. Put some small toys in a bag, (block, doll, car). Have the children take turns closing their eyes, and reach into the bag to pick a toy. Try to guess what the toy is only by touch.	**SHAPE TABLE** Most preschoolers will be able to identify a circle. Have the children go on a "circle hunt" and place on a table all the objects they can find that are shaped like a circle. Add to the table every day and review each day. Repeat the activity with squares.	**CRAFT STICK SQUARE** Give each child four craft sticks, popsicle sticks, or tongue depressors. Have the children glue them to pieces of paper in the shape of a square. With crayons, add features and turn the square into either a: TV, gift, toy box, or picture frame. Discuss what the squares could be before you pass out the crayons.	**MY OWN SHAPE BOOK** Every day the children are going to create two pages for their own shape books. Use the reproducible shape book template found on page 86. Reproduce one page per shape for each child. Today the children will each need two pages, one for a circle and one for a square.
Tuesday	**DISCUSSION TOPIC: TRIANGLES & RECTANGLES** Ask the children who can remember the names of the shapes they talked about yesterday. Who can get me a circle from the table? A square? Today the children are going to learn about **triangles** and **rectangles**. How many sides does a triangle have? A rectangle? Let's find some triangles and rectangles to put on the shape table.	**WHERE DO THE SHAPES GO?** Use a small book shelf for this activity. Ask the children to pick up an object from the shape table and place it on the bookshelf. For example: "Katie, go and get a triangle and put it on the bottom shelf." Then that child gets to give a direction, including a shape and positional direction, to another child.	**LARGE MAT BEAN BAG SHAPE GAME** Complete directions for this activity can be found on page 87.	**MY OWN SHAPE BOOK CONTINUED. . .** Today have the children make a page for a triangle and a page for a rectangle.
Wednesday	**SHOW-AND-TELL DAY WEDNESDAY** **DISCUSSION TOPIC: STARS & DIAMONDS** Ask who can remember the names of the shapes we talked about yesterday. Today the children are going to learn about **stars** and **diamonds**. Let's count. How many sides does a diamond have? A star?	**SHAPE CARDS** Use the reproducible shape cards found on page 88. Make eight copies of page 88—each copy on a different color of paper. Cut apart and laminate for durability. Use the cards two ways: sort according to color and sort according to shape.	**FLANNEL BOARD SHAPES** Cut out many shapes from felt in a wide variety of sizes and colors. Use the felt shapes like patterns blocks. The children can create pictures on a flannel board with the shapes. *(See illustrations.)*	**MY OWN SHAPE BOOK CONTINUED. . .** Today have the children make a page for a star and a page for a diamond.
Thursday	**DISCUSSION TOPIC: OVALS & OCTAGONS** Ask who can remember the names of all the shapes they learned this week. Today the children are going to learn about **ovals** and **octagons**. How many sides does an octagon have? Does an oval have any straight lines? Let's find some ovals and octagons for the shape table.	**SHAPE LACING CARDS** These can be purchased commercially or they can be easily home-made. Draw a shape on a sturdy piece of cardboard. Punch holes. Lace with a 36" piece of yarn. Wrap masking tape (1-1/2") around one end of the yarn to serve as a safe needle. Children love playing with lacing cards and can feel the shape as they lace.	**BUILD A ROBOT** Complete directions can be found on page 87.	**MY OWN SHAPE BOOK CONTINUED. . .** Today have the children make a page for an oval and a page for an octagon.
Friday	**SPECIAL NEWS FRIDAY** **DISCUSSION TOPIC: SHAPE REVIEW** Review the names of all eight shapes. Ask the children if they can identify all of the eight shapes by name?	**SHAPE PUZZLES** Use the shape cards found on page 88. Copy, color, and cut the shapes in half. Place on a table and let the children find the two halves that make the whole shape.	**WHAT IS MISSING?** Use the felt shapes that you made for the flannel board shapes activity. Place three to five shapes on the flannel board. Have the children close their eyes and then remove a shape. Have the children guess which shape is missing.	**FINISH OUR SHAPE BOOKS** Finish the shape books by adding covers. The children can decorate their covers by drawing many shapes. Bind the books by punching holes along the side, string yarn through the holes, and tie a bow. The children can take their books home and "read" them to their parents.

 Early Learning Thematic Lesson Plans

My Own Shape Book

Directions: Fill the page with shapes: construction paper, shapes cut from old magazines, or shapes that are drawn by the child.

The name of this shape is

○ _____

My shape collage

Draw the shape.

LARGE MAT BEAN BAG SHAPE GAME

You will need a discarded plastic window shade, vinyl tablecloth, or plastic shower curtain. With a permanent black marker, draw a 12-square grid with a shape in each square. Color each shape a different color. *(See illustration.)*

Give the children bean bags to toss onto the grid. They must tell you the name of the shape and its color. You can also play the game by telling the children which shape to aim for, and watch if they can toss the bean bag onto the shape that you have specified.

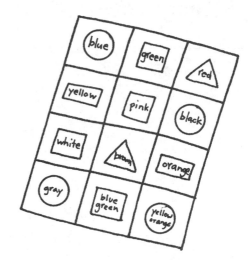

BUILD A ROBOT

You will need to prepare a spinner and a wide variety of corresponding shapes. Make a large spinner by cutting a circle out of cardboard and dividing it into eight sections. In each section of the circle, draw a shape. In the center punch a hole and, with a brass fastener, attach an arrow that spins. The arrow can be cut out from the plastic lid of a margarine or butter container. Out of cardboard, cut shapes that correspond with the shapes on the spinner. Make several of each shape in a variety of sizes. Since the goal of the game is to build a robot, cover the shapes in aluminum foil so they are shiny and "robot-like." *(See the illustrations below for ideas.)*

To play the game, the children will take turns spinning the arrow. When the arrow stops on a shape, the children will pick up that shape and begin to build the robot. If the arrow lands on a line, the child may spin again. The children may also work cooperatively to build one robot. Each time you play the game the robot looks different. Encourage the children to name the shape as they pick it up and add it to the robot.

Shape Cards Directions for using the cards are found on page 85.

circle

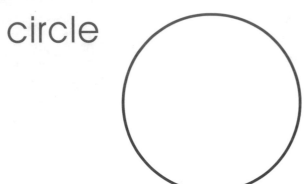

square

triangle

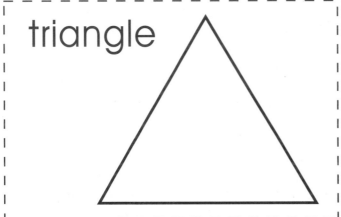

rectangle

star

diamond

oval

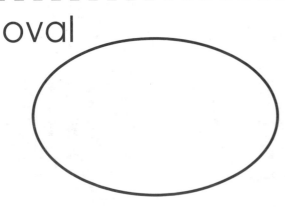

octagon

Theme 18: Somewhere Over The Rainbow! (St. Patrick's Day)

	Activity 1	Activity 2	Activity 3	Activity 4
Monday	**DISCUSSION TOPIC: ST. PATRICK** This week is called "Somewhere over the Rainbow." This means that the children are going to talk about St. Patrick's Day, leprechauns, rainbows, Ireland, fun legends, and the color green. Is anyone in our class Irish? What do we think St. Patrick's Day is all about?	**ST. PATRICK'S DAY HISTORY** The history of St. Patrick's Day can be found on page 91. Look on page 158–160 *(Children's Literature Reference Guide)* for a listing of children's books about St. Patrick's Day.	**THE SHAMROCK** Copy the shamrock pattern found on page 91 onto green construction paper. Use this pattern to make shamrock pins for the children to wear at their St. Patrick's Day party. The shamrocks can also be used to create shamrock wreaths *(paste many in a circle)* to decorate the classroom.	**HOT POTATO** Potatoes are a favorite food of the Irish. Play "hot potato" using a real potato. Have the children sit in a circle. Play some music and have the children pass the potato around the circle quickly. When the music stops, the person holding the potato gets to be the next person to start and stop the music.
Tuesday	**DISCUSSION TOPIC: LEPRECHAUNS** Yesterday the children learned about St. Patrick and the legend of why there are no snakes in Ireland. Today the children are going to learn another funny legend about the Irish little people called leprechauns. Who has ever heard of a leprechaun? Do you think leprechauns are real or pretend?	**THE LEGEND OF THE LEPRECHAUN** Read the children the story of *The Legend of the Leprechaun* found on page 90. After the story, provide the children with a copy of the leprechaun found on page 90. Enlarge the pattern for the children to color. Use for retelling the story.	**WHERE'S MY GOLD?** One child is chosen to be the leprechaun. The leprechaun closes their eyes while the teacher gives another child a small pot of gold to hide behind their back. The leprechaun may ask three "yes" or "no" questions to figure out who has the gold. For example: Is it a girl? Is the person wearing red?	**IF I HAD THREE WISHES** Besides leprechauns, there are many Irish tales about fairies. Some of the stories say that if you catch a fairy she must grant you three wishes. If you caught a fairy, what would you wish for? Write down the children's responses and place them on a bulletin board under the caption, "My Three Wishes."
Wednesday	**SHOW-AND-TELL DAY WEDNESDAY** **DISCUSSION TOPIC: RAINBOWS** Yesterday the children learned about leprechauns. Ask who can remember where the leprechaun hid his pot of gold. Today we are going to learn more about rainbows.	**REAL RAINBOWS** Rainbows are not pretend. We really can see rainbows in the sky. Bring in a prism and show the children how the light shines through and creates a rainbow. If it is nice and sunny outside, turn the outside water on and hold the hose up to the sun. The children will be able to see another real rainbow.	**RAINBOW COLORS** Discuss rainbows with the children. What colors can you see in a rainbow? Give each child a circular paper coffee filter. Fill an ice cube tray or a muffin tin with water. Add food coloring to each section. With eyedroppers, let the children drop colors onto the filter and watch as the colors blend together.	**SOMEWHERE OVER THE RAINBOW** Play the song "*Over the Rainbow*" for the children. *The Wizard of Oz* is still a popular movie, so many of the children may have already heard the song. Teach the children to sing "*Over the Rainbow.*"
Thursday	**DISCUSSION TOPIC: IRISH LEGENDS** Who has heard of the **Blarney Stone**? This is another story from Ireland. The Queen of England wanted to take land from the Irish Lord of Blarney. The Lord of Blarney could not speak very well, which made him worry that he would not be able to convince to the Queen to allow him to keep his land. The Lord of Blarney met an old woman and he shared his worries with her. The old woman told him about a special magic stone that was built into the Lord's castle wall. If he kissed that special stone, he would receive the gift of speech. The Lord of Blarney kissed the stone and was able to convince the Queen that he should keep his land. To this day, they say that whoever kisses the blarney stone will receive good luck.		**PAINTED ROCKS** Have each of the children bring a rock to school. Let them paint their rocks. When the paint is dry, spray with a gloss fixative. Let the children name their stones, just like the blarney stone has a name. Encourage them to try and make up a story about their stone.	**PASS THE BLARNEY STONE** Have the children sit in a circle and pass around a rock. The first child who holds the rock begins a story with one sentence. The next child holds the rock and adds to the story. Keep passing the rock and have the children add to the story.
Friday	**SPECIAL NEWS FRIDAY** **PARTY:** It is the day of the St. Patrick's Day party, so make some mischief the night before to surprise the children. Put shamrocks and paper gold coins all around the room and rearrange the furniture. Make it look as if a leprechaun had been there.	**LEPRECHAUN HAT** Have each of the children make a leprechaun hat to wear to the party. Hats can be made from black construction paper with a green paper shamrock glued to the front.	**PIN THE POT UNDER THE RAINBOW** This is a fun party game, played just like "Pin the tail on the donkey," Draw a large rainbow and a small leprechaun on a sheet of paper or on the blackboard. Make a pot of gold for each child. Let the children take turns wearing a blindfold and trying to place their pot next to the leprechaun.	**LEPRECHAUN SHAKES** An exciting treat to make for the party are "leprechaun shakes." Simply put peppermint bon bon ice cream and a splash of milk in a blender. Top with a spoonful of whipped cream and serve in paper cups with plastic spoons.

The Legend of the Leprechaun

Describe the leprechaun to the children before reading the story. Describe what the leprechaun looks like and his personality traits. This will help the children to better understand the story. Here is the information: A leprechaun is an Irish fairy who looks like a very little old man. They say he is about two feet tall. (Use a yard stick and show the children how tall two feet is.) They also say that he is grouchy, has very poor manners, likes to live alone, and enjoys making shoes whenever he is not getting into trouble.

Once upon a time, on a far away island called Ireland, lived a very little, very clever, and very grouchy leprechaun. This particular leprechaun lived in a cottage deep in the forest where no one could bother him. The leprechaun preferred to live alone, and made shoes to pass the time. Although the cottage was well hidden, the people in the village knew that the leprechaun lived close by.

Year after year, the people would go into the forest and search for the leprechaun. And year after year, they never found him. Occasionally someone would hear the tapping of his little hammer, but no one had ever been able to catch him. The people in the village really wanted to catch the leprechaun. All the village people believed that the leprechaun had hidden a pot of gold under the rainbow and that the leprechaun was the only one who knew how to get under the rainbow. They also believed that the leprechaun had to give the gold to the person who caught him!

One day, the kind and gentle toy maker went for a walk along the forest path. Suddenly, he heard the tap-tap-tapping of the leprechaun's little hammer. Quietly, the toy maker followed the tapping sound. As the toy maker stood behind a large tree he could see the tiny leprechaun busy hammering his shoes. The toy maker jumped out from behind the tree and yelled, "Leprechaun, I caught you!"

An angry and surprised leprechaun replied, "Aye, ya did! Follow me and I'll take ya to under the rainbow and to me pot of gold."

The leprechaun and the toy maker set off and walked for many, many miles. Finally, the two were actually standing in a beautiful huge field of bright green bushes under the rainbow. The leprechaun pointed to the spot where the pot of gold was buried. The toy maker said, "I have to dig to get the pot of gold and I do not have a shovel. I will have to go home to get a shovel and come back to dig out the pot of gold."

The toy maker was also a clever man. All the bushes in the field looked exactly the same. The toy maker knew it would be difficult to remember where the pot of gold was buried. So to help him remember, the toy maker took off his red scarf and tied it on the bush that marked the spot where the pot of gold was buried. The toy maker thanked the grouchy leprechaun and set off for home to get his shovel, and the grouchy leprechaun scampered back to his home.

The toy maker returned home, grabbed his shovel, and began his long walk back to under the rainbow. When the toy maker reached the field he was shocked by what he saw! He did not see his one red scarf. He saw thousands of red scarfs! There was a red scarf on every bush in the field. He had no idea where to start digging! It would be impossible to find the pot of gold. That leprechaun had outsmarted him! And that is the legend of the leprechaun!

(Enlarge and photocopy the leprechaun for the children to color.)

The History of St. Patrick's Day

(St. Patrick's Day was originally a Catholic Holy Day that has evolved into a more secular holiday. The following history is for your reference. If you teach in a Christian school, you may wish to share the religious aspects of the history of St. Patrick. If you teach in a public school, you can adapt the information to what you feel is appropriate for your school setting.)

HISTORY: St. Patrick's Day is celebrated everywhere on March 17 by both Irish and non-Irish people. It is a day filled with parades, wonderful music, boiled beef and cabbage feasts, and, of course, shamrocks and the traditional wearing of green.

St. Patrick, the patron saint of Ireland, was a man whose name is believed to have been Maewyn Succat. He was born around 385 A.D. He was not born in Ireland, but probably in either Wales or Scotland. When he was only sixteen years old, he was sold into slavery in Ireland. During his six years in slavery he was a shepherd. Maewyn studied and discovered a deep faith while in captivity. He escaped and eventually returned to Ireland as a missionary. He organized schools, churches, and was able to convert many people to Christianity.

THE SHAMROCK: The shamrock is a traditional symbol for St. Patrick's Day. It is believed that St. Patrick used this symbol when he taught about the Holy Trinity. He used it as a visual to describe how the Father, the Son, and the Holy Spirit could all be one in the same. The shamrock has become a symbol for this holiday celebration. It is also symbolic of the beautiful green countryside in Ireland. There is a myth in Ireland that everything good comes in threes. The shamrock, with its three leaves, is a symbol of good luck.

NO-SNAKES IN IRELAND: St. Patrick spent thirty years in Ireland and is credited for converting most of the country's population. There are many tales about the power of his work, but few are actually substantiated. The most well-known tale that is fun to explore with a classroom of children is the story of how St. Patrick spoke from a hilltop and drove all the snakes out of Ireland. The snakes supposedly all fell into the sea. The remarkable part of the story is that there really are no snakes in Ireland!

A Shamrock Pattern

Theme 19: The Greatest Show On Earth (Circus)

	Activity 1	Activity 2	Activity 3	Activity 4
Monday	**DISCUSSION TOPIC: CIRCUS** This week the children are going to learn about the circus and actually become circus performers. The children have a lot to do this week to get ready. *(Send home the circus invitation to the children's families. Invitation found on page 96.)*	**READ ABOUT THE CIRCUS** Use the Children's Literature Guide found on pages 158–160 as a reference for good children's books about the circus. Share several stories with the children. Talk about what they learned from the stories. Leave the books on a table for the children to look at during free moments.	**ADVERTISING POSTERS** Provide each of the children with an 11"x17" piece of white paper. Let the children create an illustration about the circus. Add the date, place, and time for the circus performance. Display around the school.	**THE CIRCUS PARADE SONG** The children will begin and end the show with *"The Circus Parade Song"* found on page 95. Begin teaching and practicing the song.
Tuesday	**DISCUSSION TOPIC: COSTUMES & PROPS** Today is costume day. The children are going to make all of their costumes. (Organize the children into their specific acts before creating costumes. Look at page 93 for a list of the characters.)	**MAKE COSTUMES** Spend a good part of the day helping the children create their costumes for the circus. Plan ahead and organize the materials you will need. Costume and prop directions are found on page 93.		**MORE PRACTICE** Practice *"The Circus Parade Song"* found on page 95.
Wednesday	**SHOW-AND-TELL DAY WEDNESDAY** **REHEARSALS:** Tell the children that today is the first day of circus rehearsals. Plan independent activities so you can work with each of the acts individually. Begin with the ringmaster. (Ringmaster performance—Ideas are found on page 94.)	**ACT 1 THE LIONS & LION TAMER** Ideas are found on page 94. **ACT 2 THE ELEPHANTS** Ideas are found on page 94.	**ACT 3 THE ACROBATS** Ideas are found on page 94. **ACT 4 THE CLOWNS** Ideas are found on page 94.	**ACT 5 THE STRONG PEOPLE** Ideas are found on page 95. **ACT 6 THE TIGHTROPE WALKERS** Ideas are found on pages 94–95. **MORE PRACTICE** Practice *"The Circus Parade Song"* found on page 95.
Thursday	**DISCUSSION TOPIC: MORE REHEARSALS** The majority of the day will be spent in rehearsals. Make this a fun and successful experience for the children. Spend part of the day decorating. Add balloons and streamers to your classroom.	**INDIVIDUAL PRACTICE** Spend part of the day allowing each of the groups to practice individually. Explain to the children that first they will practice alone, and then everyone will perform the entire circus.	**PRACTICE THE ENTIRE SHOW** Spend time putting the entire show together. Begin with the beginning circus parade and song and end with the song. Go through the entire show at least twice. Tomorrow is the big day. Help the children feel secure in the fact that they are ready to perform.	**POPCORN BAGS** End the day by allowing the children to decorate small brown lunch bags. These bags will be used tomorrow for the popcorn.
Friday	**SPECIAL NEWS FRIDAY** **DISCUSSION TOPIC: CIRCUS DAY** It is the big day for "The Greatest Show on Earth."	**POPCORN AND LEMONADE** Have your volunteers pop the popcorn. The children can help fill the decorated bags with popcorn. Make the lemonade and refrigerate until show time.	**COSTUMES AND MAKE-UP** Have all the children get in their costumes. Have the volunteers ready to help children with their make up. Is everyone ready? It is almost show time!	**"THE GREATEST SHOW ON EARTH" PERFORMANCE** It's show time! At the end of the performance serve the popcorn and lemonade to the audience and the cast!

The Circus Costumes and Props

THE CIRCUS CHARACTERS—WHO WILL YOU BE?

Divide the children into six circus acts and choose one child to be the ringmaster.

You will need: a ringmaster

Act 1: Multiple lions and one lion tamer

Act 2: Elephants and an elephant trainer

Act 3: Several acrobats

Act 4: Several clowns

Act 5: Several tightrope walkers

Act 6: Several strongmen/women

HOW TO MAKE A PILLOWCASE COSTUME

Each child will wear a pillowcase costume. Cut openings for the child's head and two arm holes. Decorate by painting designs with fabric paint. *(See illustration.)*

THE RINGMASTER

In the letter sent home to the parents *(page 96)*, a sports coat for the ringmaster was requested. Add a top hat made from black construction paper and a microphone. Wrap paper around the cardboard center from a roll of paper towels.

LIONS

Ask the children that will be lions to wear brown clothing on the day of the circus. Fabric paint *(or dye)* a brown pillow case for each lion. Make "manes" with brown and gold crepe paper. Cut fringe that fits the entire way around the child's head. Hoola hoops are great for the lions to jump through and small stools are good for the lions to stand on. *(The elephants will also use the stools.)* Add whiskers with an eye brow pencil.

LION TAMER AND ELEPHANT TRAINER

The lion tamer can decorate his pillowcase with a painted picture of a lion or things that are seen in the jungle. The elephant trainer can decorate his pillowcase with a painted picture of an elephant or things that are seen in the jungle. The lion tamer will also need a small whip to direct the lions. (Attach multi-colored strips of crepe paper to a 12" ruler, to make a friendly whip.)

ELEPHANTS

Have the children dress in grey and black on the day of the circus. Create giant elephant ears by making construction paper headbands to fit each child's head. Staple large gray elephant ear cut-outs to the head bands. Paint the elephants' pillowcases gray. Use stools for the elephants' tricks.

CLOWNS AND A CLOWN CAR

Paint each of the clowns' pillowcases with bright colors and add polka-dots, stripes, smile faces, buttons, or big bows. Use make up to create a clown face. To make a funny car for the clown act, use a large box and paint it to resemble a car. Cut out the back of the box (passenger's side). Make a door that opens on the driver's side of the car.

ACROBATS

The acrobats should wear shorts under their pillowcase costumes. Fabric paint the pillow-cases with bright colors. Tie a scarf around each acrobat's waist. Tumbling mats will be needed for this performance.

STRONGMEN/WOMEN

The pillowcase costumes can have barbells painted on the front. To make barbells for the performance, tape a blown-up balloon on each end of a yardstick. Each strong person should have his own barbells.

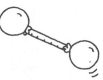

TIGHTROPE WALKERS

The tightrope walkers should wear tights under their pillowcase costumes. Fabric paint them with bright colors. Tie a scarf around each acrobat's waist. Each tightrope walker will need an umbrella. Use a short balance beam or create an imaginary masking tape tightrope.

Directions for The Circus Acts

AS PEOPLE ARRIVE
    Locate some fun circus-type music to play as people are arriving. Have two children welcome the people and show them where to sit.

THE CIRCUS OPENING PARADE
    All the children will be singing *"The Circus Parade Song."* The children should enter the room when they hear their verse. For example, the ringmaster is the first who enters. He steps forward when the children begin to sing, "The ringmaster announces the acts..." Proceed until all the children have entered and paraded around the room.

*(**Ringmaster** —Announces Act One – the lions and the lion tamer.)*

ACT ONE – THE LIONS AND THE LION TAMER
    The lions should enter, acting fierce and roaring. The lion tamer should crack his crepe paper whip and direct the lions to stand in a row. Once the lions have lined up, the tamer should direct them to jump through a hoop one at a time. *(Encourage the crowd to cheer!)* They end their performance with the poem: **"The lion is the jungle king. He takes care of his pride. He watches over all the beasts. His roar makes them hide."** The tamer should direct the animals out of the ring.

*(**Ringmaster** —Announces Act Two – the elephants and the elephant trainer.)*

ACT TWO – THE ELEPHANTS AND ELEPHANT TRAINER
    Circus music should be playing in the background. The elephant trainer leads the elephants into the ring. The elephants enter swinging their trunks *(hold arms straight and hold hands together)*. They follow the trainer around the ring. Each elephant will need his own stool. The trainer should instruct each elephant to stand on the stool, sit on the stool, walk around the stool, then put one foot up on the stool. *(Encourage the crowd to cheer.)* The elephants should speak and act out the poem: **"All the elephants went out to play. Swinging and swaying their trunks. They stomped and stomped all day long. Finally, they laid down, kerplunk!"** The trainer should then direct the elephants out of the ring.

*(**Ringmaster** —Announces Act Three – the acrobats.)*

ACT THREE – THE ACROBATS
    Place tumbling mats down. The acrobats should come running in and perform somersaults on the mats. Pre-determine the skill levels of the children who were chosen to be the acrobats. Let each child perform a couple of tumbling sequences alone *(probably just somersaults).* The acrobats should end their performance by lining up and performing a somersault at the same time.

*(**Ringmaster** —Announces Act Four – the clowns.)*

ACT FOUR – THE CLOWNS
    Place the clown car in front of the audience. The clowns should enter through the car door one at a time. If possible, have the children circle and come through the car a couple of times—this will give the illusion of many clowns coming out of the car. When all the clowns have come out of the car three times, have them tell a couple of jokes. **Joke one: "Knock, knock. Who's there? Boo. Boo who? Don't cry!" Joke two: "Why do elephants wear tennis shoes? So they won't hurt their feet jumping out of trees!"**

*(**Ringmaster** —Announces Act Five – the tightrope walkers.)*

ACT FIVE – THE TIGHTROPE WALKERS

Use a balance beam or make a masking tape beam on the floor. The tightrope walkers should walk in on tiptoe holding their umbrellas high. The performers should sit on the beam, stand with two feet on the beam, stand on their left feet, right feet, walk backwards, walk forward, turn in a circle, jump off! Put hands up in the air just like in the Olympics! The children should walk off to music playing. The tightrope walkers might also think it is fun to walk on stilts. You can make stilts with ropes and small coffee cans. Punch a hole on either side of the coffee can and tie rope for the child to use as a handle.

*(**Ringmaster** —Announces Act Six – the strong people.)*

ACT SIX – THE STRONG PEOPLE

The barbells should be set in the ring ready for the strong people. The strong people enter the ring, show off their muscles, and parade around the ring. They will stop in front of a barbell and one at a time, each child will take their turn lifting the barbell and showing off their strength. The children should struggle and make it look as if the barbells are really heavy.

*(**Ringmaster** —Closes the show and thanks the audience for coming.)*

THE FINALE

End the circus with the entire cast parading around the classroom, singing *"The Circus Parade Song."* Encourage cheering and applause!

 The Circus Parade Song
(Sung to the tune of "The Wheels on the Bus.")

The circus is here, let's stand and cheer. Stand and cheer. Stand and Cheer.
The circus is here, let's stand and cheer. We love the circus!

The ringmaster in the circus announces the acts. Announces the acts. Announces the acts.
The ringmaster in the circus announces the acts. We love the circus!

The lions in the circus go roar, roar, roar. Roar, roar, roar. Roar, roar, roar.
The lions in the circus go roar, roar, roar. We love the circus!

The elephants in the circus swing their trunks. Swing their trunks. Swing their trunks.
The elephants in the circus swing their trunks. We love the circus!

The acrobats in the circus tumble and tumble. Tumble and tumble. Tumble and tumble.
The acrobats in the circus tumble and tumble. We love the circus!

The clowns in the circus make us laugh. Make us laugh. Make us laugh.
The clowns in the circus make us laugh. We love the circus!

The strongmen in the circus lift big weights. Lift big weights. Lift big weights.
The strongmen in the circus lift big weights. We love the circus!

The tightrope walkers in the circus walk on tip-toes. Walk on tip-toes. Walk on tip-toes.
The tightrope walkers in the circus walk on tip-toes. We love the circus!

The circus is here, let's stand and cheer. Stand and cheer. Stand and Cheer.
The circus is here, let's stand and cheer. We love the circus!

This is an invitation to
"The Greatest Show on Earth!"

Date:_____

Dear Parents and Family Members,

   This week our class is learning about the circus! At the end of the week we are going to be performing in our own circus, complete with clowns, lions, tigers, acrobats, elephants, a ringmaster, tightrope walkers, and even a strongman! We would love the parents and any other family members to attend.

We hope that you will be able to come and see our "GREATEST SHOW ON EARTH!"

When: _____

Where: _____

ALL THE CHILDREN NEED TO BRING AN OLD PILLOWCASE TO SCHOOL. WE ARE TURNING THE OLD PILLOWCASES INTO COSTUMES. PLEASE SEND TO SCHOOL TOMORROW. IF YOU CAN SPARE TWO, THAT WOULD BE WONDERFUL!)

- -

We also need some help from our parents.

We need some props for our circus. Please check any of the following you can provide.

_____ Donate popcorn and instant lemonade
_____ Umbrellas for the tightrope walkers
_____ Sports coat for the Ringmaster
_____ Make up for the clowns
_____ Hoola hoops for the lions to jump through
_____ Crepe paper or party streamers
_____ Funny hats, shoes, and ribbons for the clowns
_____ Yardsticks
_____ Balloons

We will need some help on the day of the circus. If you can provide any of the following assistance, please check the box and return this form to school with your child.

_____ I can help with make up and hair.
_____ I can help with putting on clown make up.
_____ I can help serve popcorn and lemonade.
_____ I can help with clean up.
_____ I can take pictures during the performance.

Family name: _____

Theme 20: Let's Go Fly A Kite (Weather)

	Activity 1	Activity 2	Activity 3	Activity 4
Monday	**DISCUSSION: WEATHER WEEK** This week the unit is called, "Let's go fly a kite." Ask the children what they think that means. Explain that one needs windy weather to fly a kite and that the children are going to learn about weather. Make a list of all the weather words that we know.	**CLASSROOM WEATHER CHART** Make a classroom weather chart (see example) where the children can graph the weather every day. Make comparisons. Try to predict what the weather might be like. WEATHER S M T W T F S	**MY OWN PERSONAL WEATHER CHART** Use the reproducible activity found on page 98. Copy, color, cut out, and glue onto a paper plate. Punch a small hole in the center and attach the two arrows with a brass fastener. Two arrows are included because two weather conditions often exist, such as, sunny and hot, or cold and rainy.	**MY FAVORITE WEATHER** Use the list of weather words that the children came up with earlier in the day. Ask the children to vote for their favorite weather. Discuss all the types of activities that can be played in each weather condition from sledding to swimming.
Tuesday	**DISCUSSION TOPIC: WIND** Wind is a difficult concept for children. Ask them what they think wind is. **EXPERIMENT:** Bring to school a large empty jar or a large shell. Listen to the sound made by an empty jar or shell. Many people say it sounds like ocean waves. Air actually makes sounds. Now fill the jar with water and listen. Surprise, the sound is gone!	**LIONS AND LAMBS** In the spring, we hear the old saying, "In like a lion and out like a lamb." Explain to the children what this saying means. On page 99 is a reproducible lion and lamb for the children to color.	**LET'S FLY A KITE** Bring a real kite to school, hopefully on a windy day. Many young children have never had the experience of watching a real kite fly in the air. This is also a good time to talk about power lines and why we must never fly kites near power lines.	**LET'S MAKE WIND** Fold a piece of construction paper into an accordion fan. Have the children wave their fans and feel the wind. Teach the children to fold paper planes and take them outside to fly.
Wednesday	**SHOW-AND-TELL DAY WEDNESDAY** **DISCUSSION TOPIC: RAIN** Teach the children the verse, "Rain, rain, go away, Come again another day. Little _____ wants to play."	**MAKE RAIN IN THE CLASSROOM** How exciting to make it rain in the classroom! Fill a tea kettle with water and heat. Hold an empty jar over the spout of the kettle. The jar will fill with steam (which looks like clouds), and because the jar is cool, the steam inside the jar will form droplets, then fall out just like rain!	**RAINY DAY PICTURES** Have each child draw and color a picture that includes clouds. When the picture is finished, have the children drip white glue drops onto the picture. The glue will dry clear and look like raindrops.	**PUDDLE JUMPING** Make light blue construction paper puddles. Print a number on each puddle. Say a number and have the children jump to the correct puddle. The puddles can also be arranged like a hopscotch pattern.
Thursday	**DISCUSSION TOPIC: CLOUDY AND COLD** Some children do not like cloudy and rainy days because they cannot go outside and play. Make a list of all the fun games you can play inside on those cold wet days.	**WHAT DO YOU SEE?** On a cloudy day, take the children outside and have them lay down and look at the clouds. What do they see? Encourage them to use their imaginations.	**CLOUD PICTURES** Give each of the children a piece of construction paper, glue, and some cotton balls. Tell the children to glue the cotton into some cloud shape. When they looked at the clouds did they see a dinosaur? A cat? A house?	**AN INDOOR PICNIC** How much fun to have an indoor picnic on a cold and rainy day! Put blankets on the floor and pretend that you are outside. Use paper plates, sing songs, and play games where you pretend to be seeing different outdoor things, such as ants, dogs running, baseball games, etc.
Friday	**SPECIAL NEWS FRIDAY** **DISCUSSION TOPIC: SUNNY AND HOT/ALL WEATHER CONDITIONS** Make a list of great outside games that you can play on a warm and sunny day.	**WEATHER PUZZLES** Find pictures in old magazines that show a variety of weather conditions. Mount the pictures on cardboard and cut into pieces. The children will have fun reassembling the weather puzzles.	**IT'S WARM OUTSIDE** On a warm day, bring the children outside with pails or pans of water. Let them experiment with things that float or sink. Give them aluminum foil and ask them to make a boat that floats. The foil boat creations can be impressive.	**MAKE A WEATHER SCENE** Complete directions for this activity are found on page 100.

My Own Personal Weather Chart

Reproduce for each child in your class. Color, cut out, and glue onto a paper plate.
Punch a hole and attach the two arrows with a brass fastener.

The Windy Lion and The Quiet Lamb

Color.

99

Make a Weather Scene

Look at the little house and all the weather pictures at the bottom of the page.
Color the picture and then use the weather pictures as a guide for drawing your own.

Use these pictures to give you ideas about what to draw in your scene.

Theme 21: Things That Make Me Feel Good! (Self-Esteem)

	Activity 1	Activity 2	Activity 3	Activity 4
Monday	**DISCUSSION TOPIC: I AM SPECIAL** This week the children are going to talk about themselves and all the reasons why they are special. Go around the group and ask the children to tell what they like best about themselves and what they are good at.	**SAME AND DIFFERENT** Talk about all the ways that people are the same and all the ways that people can be different. Stress how wonderful it is that we are all different. Make a graph about your class. Graph eye and hair color, height, number of siblings, pets, or favorite toys. Discuss how our differences make us special.	**MY OWN SPECIAL BOOK** Over the next few days the children are going to make small books entitled, "My Own Special Book." Each day they will add a few pages that provide all sorts of fun information about the child.	**MY OWN SPECIAL BOOK CONTINUED....** Begin the project, "My Own Special Book." Complete the cover and page 2, "This is me," found on page 102.
Tuesday	**DISCUSSION TOPIC: THINGS THAT MAKE ME HAPPY** Talk with the children about all the things that make them happy. Make a list. **BABY PICTURES** Send notes home with the children that request that each child bring a baby picture to school on Friday to share.	**MY OWN SPECIAL BOOK CONTINUED....** Complete page 3, "This is my school," found on page 102. **SING THE SONG** *"If You're Happy and You Know It."*	**MY OWN SPECIAL BOOK CONTINUED....** Complete page 4, "This is my family," found on page 102.	**WE ARE SPECIAL BULLETIN BOARD** Use the reproducible activity found on page 105. Take Polaroid or digital photographs of the children and then mount them on construction paper. Below each photograph the teacher writes a statement about why the child is so special. The children will be thrilled with their teacher's personal comments.
Wednesday	**SHOW-AND-TELL DAY WEDNESDAY** **DISCUSSION TOPIC: I AM SPECIAL** Learn the rhyme: Look in the mirror, What do you see? Someone special! Yes, it's me!	**MY OWN SPECIAL BOOK CONTINUED....** Complete page 5, "This is my house," found on page 103.	**MY OWN SPECIAL BOOK CONTINUED....** Complete page 6, "These are my friends," found on page 103.	**MY OWN SPECIAL BOOK CONTINUED....** Complete page 7, "My favorite thing to do at school is...," found on page 103.
Thursday	**DISCUSSION TOPIC: THINGS THAT MAKE ME SAD** Talk with the children about all of the things that make them sad. The teacher should be sure to share, too!	**MY OWN SPECIAL BOOK CONTINUED....** Complete page 8, "My favorite animal is...," found on page 103.	**ALL ABOUT ME POSTER** Have each child create an "All About Me" poster. They can draw a picture of themselves and add some of their favorite things. Have the children take turns sharing their posters with the rest of the class.	**MY OWN SPECIAL BOOK CONTINUED....** Complete page 9, "I am very good at...," found on page 104.
Friday	**SPECIAL NEWS FRIDAY** **DISCUSSION TOPIC: WE ARE GROWING UP** Talk with the children about how they are each growing up and learning to do more and more things. Ask them, "What can you do now that you could not do when you were a baby?"	**MY OWN SPECIAL BOOK CONTINUED....** Complete page 10, "This is my favorite toy," found on page 104. **SHARE BABY PICTURES** Let the children take turns sharing their baby pictures. What were their first words? When did they learn to walk? Discuss how much they have learned.	**MY OWN SPECIAL BOOK CONTINUED....** Complete page 11, "If I had one wish, I would wish for...," found on page 104.	**MY OWN SPECIAL BOOK CONTINUED....** Complete page 12, "When I grow up I want to be...," found on page 104. Now place all the pages together and staple in numerical order.

My Own Special Book

My Own Special Book

-1-

This is me.

My name is

_____

-2-

This is my school.

-3-

This is my family.

-4-

My Own Special Book

This is my house.

-5-

These are my friends.

-6-

My favorite thing to do at school is

_____.

-7-

My favorite animal is

_____.

-8-

My Own Special Book

I am very good at

_____ .

-9-

This is my favorite toy,

-10-

If I had one wish,
I would wish for

_____ .

-11-

When I grow up,
I want to be

_____ .

-12-

My teacher thinks I am special because:

_____

_____

_____

Theme 22: We Love Mother Goose! (Nursery Rhymes)

	Activity 1	Activity 2	Activity 3	Activity 4
Monday	**DISCUSSION TOPIC: NURSERY RHYMES** This week the children are going to learn some nursery rhymes. Find out what nursery rhymes the children already know. Nursery rhymes are effective tools for teaching some basic concepts. **TODAY'S NURSERY RHYMES:** *Twinkle, Twinkle Little Star and Humpty Dumpty*	**TWINKLE, TWINKLE LITTLE STAR** Discuss the concept of "up." Stars are "up" in the sky. Give each child a black piece of paper and white glue. Put drops of glue on the paper and sprinkle with glitter. Practice saying the rhyme.	**HUMPTY DUMPTY** Humpty Dumpty falls "down." Discuss the concept of "down." Make Humpty Dumpty number puzzles that can be put back together again. Complete directions are found on page 110.	**MY NURSERY RHYME COLORING BOOK** Reproduce pages 107–109 for each child in your class. Cut along the dotted lines and staple in numerical order "My Nursery Rhyme Coloring Book" for each child. Every day this week, the children will color two pages that match the two rhymes they learned that day. Today complete the cover and pages 2 and 3.
Tuesday	**DISCUSSION TOPIC: REVIEW** Review the rhymes the children learned yesterday. Today's rhymes also teach the concepts of "up and down." Teach the new rhymes. **TODAY'S NURSERY RHYMES:** *Hickory Dickory Dock and Jack and Jill*	**HICKORY DICKORY DOCK** Review concepts of "up and down," as well as counting to 12. Show the children a clock and count the numbers. Change the rhyme. Substitute "one" for other numbers, for example "the clock struck 5" and have the children clap 5 times. Let the children make their own clock. Complete directions found on page 110.	**JACK AND JILL** As you say the rhyme, let the children have the fun of acting it out. Jack and Jill went up the hill to fetch a pail of water. Provide experiences where the children experiment with the concept of filling containers so they are "full" and "empty."	**MY NURSERY RHYME COLORING BOOK Continued . . .** Color pages 4 and 5 of "My Nursery Rhyme Coloring Book."
Wednesday	**SHOW-AND-TELL DAY WEDNESDAY** **DISCUSSION TOPIC: REVIEW** Review the rhymes that children have learned so far. Introduce and teach the new rhymes and the concepts of "little, big, and beside." **TODAY'S NURSERY RHYMES:** *Little Miss Muffet and Little Bo Peep*	**LITTLE MISS MUFFET** This is another fun rhyme for the children to act out. They will love being "frightened away." Let the children make spiders using the directions on page 110. When the spiders are finished, use them to demonstrate the concept of "beside." For example, "Put your spider beside the bookshelf."	**LITTLE BO BEEP** Both Miss Muffet and Bo Peep are little. Fill a bag with pictures of things that are big and things that are little. Let the children put their hands in the bag, pull out a picture, and then tell everyone whether it is big or little. Complete directions for making Little Bo Peep and her lost sheep can be found on page 110.	**MY NURSERY RHYME COLORING BOOK Continued . . .** Color pages 6 and 7 of "My Nursery Rhyme Coloring Book."
Thursday	**DISCUSSION TOPIC: REVIEW** Once again review all the rhymes. Today's rhymes teach the concept of "over." **TODAY'S NURSERY RHYMES:** *Jack Be Nimble and Hey Diddle Diddle*	**JACK BE NIMBLE** Act out the rhyme. Set up a pretend candle to jump over. Discuss safety and that children should not jump over any real candles. Let the children create their own Jack Be Nimble picture with a real candle. Complete directions are found on page 110.	**HEY DIDDLE DIDDLE** Let the children create new rhymes by filling in the blanks. Hey diddle, diddle, The _____ and the _____. The _____ jumped Over the _____. The little _____ laughed To see such sport, And the _____ ran away With the _____.	**MY NURSERY RHYME COLORING BOOK Continued . . .** Color pages 8 and 9 of "My Nursery Rhyme Coloring Book."
Friday	**SPECIAL NEWS FRIDAY** **DISCUSSION TOPIC: REVIEW** Review all the rhymes the children have learned this week. Today's rhymes teach the concepts of "corner, in and out." **TODAY'S NURSERY RHYMES:** *Little Jack Horner and Baa, Baa, Black Sheep*	**LITTLE JACK HORNER** This is a wonderful rhyme for teaching the concepts of "corner, in and out." Have the children locate all sorts of corners in your classroom, such as table corners, block corners, or wall corners. Once again, this is a fun rhyme to pantomime.	**BAA, BAA, BLACK SHEEP** Say the rhyme and change the color of the sheep. For example, "Baa, baa, pink sheep..." Use the sheep pattern provided on page 110 to make 11 different sheep cards—each sheep a different color: red, blue, yellow, orange, green, purple, white, pink, gray, brown, and black.	**COMPLETE MY NURSERY RHYME COLORING BOOK** Color pages 10 through 12 of "My Nursery Rhyme Coloring Book." Let the children take their books home to share with their parents.

My Nursery Rhyme Coloring Book

Name _____

-1-

TWINKLE, TWINKLE LITTLE STAR
Twinkle, twinkle little star,
How I wonder what you are.
Up above the world so high,
Like a diamond in the sky.
Twinkle, twinkle little star,
How I wonder what you are.

-2-

HUMPTY DUMPTY
Humpty Dumpty sat on a wall,
Humpty Dumpty had a great fall.
All the King's horses,
And all the King's men,
Couldn't put Humpty together again.

-3-

HICKORY DICKORY DOCK
Hickory dickory dock.
The mouse ran up the clock.
The clock struck one.
The mouse ran down.
Hickory dickory dock.

-4-

JACK AND JILL
Jack and Jill went up the hill,
To fetch a pail of water.
Jack fell down and broke his crown,
And Jill came tumbling after.

-5-

LITTLE MISS MUFFET
Little Miss Muffet sat on a tuffet,
Eating her curds and whey.
Along came a spider,
And sat down beside her,
And frightened Miss Muffet away!

-6-

LITTLE BO PEEP
Little Bo Peep has lost her sheep,
And can't tell where to find them.
Leave them alone and they'll come home,
Wagging their tails behind them.

-7-

JACK BE NIMBLE
Jack be nimble,
Jack be quick.
Jack jumps over the candlestick.

-8-

HEY DIDDLE DIDDLE
Hey diddle diddle,
The cat and the fiddle,
The cow jumped over the moon;
The little dog laughed
To see such sport,
And the dish ran away with the spoon.

-9-

LITTLE JACK HORNER
Little Jack Horner sat in a corner,
Eating his Christmas pie;
He put in his thumb,
And pulled out a plum,
And said, "What a good boy am I!"

-10-

BAA, BAA, BLACK SHEEP
Baa, baa, black sheep have you any wool?
Yes sir, yes sir, three bags full.
One for my master,
and one for my dame,
And one for the little boy
Who lives down the lane.
Baa, baa, black sheep have you any wool?
Yes sir, yes sir, three bags full.

-11-

**Draw your favorite
nursery rhyme character.**

-12-

HUMPTY DUMPTY NUMBER PUZZLES

Use the illustration next to this activity as a guide to make Humpty Dumpty puzzle cards. Write a numeral on Humpty's head and then draw the corresponding number of buttons on his vest. Cut in two and let the children match the button set to the correct numeral.

HICKORY DICKORY DOCK CLOCKS

Let each of the children make their own clocks. Give each child a paper plate. Show the children where to print the numbers. If you teach a classroom of young preschoolers you will want to print the numbers on the clocks for the children. Cut arrows from margarine container lids. With brass fasteners attach the arrows to the clocks. Use the clocks to help the children identify the numbers one to twelve and to tell time on the hour.

LITTLE MISS MUFFET SPIDERS

These are easy-to-make spiders. Give each child a black construction paper circle and four black pipe cleaners. Glue the pipe cleaners across the center of the black circle. Let the glue dry and then bend the pipe cleaners to resemble spider legs. Add wiggly-eyes for a fun extra touch. These eyes can be found at most craft stores.

LITTLE BO PEEP'S LOST SHEEP

Give each child a paper with the outline of a sheep. Brush diluted white glue *(2 parts glue, 1 part water)* on the inside of the sheep outline, and fill the center with cotton. Talk about how "soft" the cotton is. What are some other things that are soft? What are some things that are hard?

JACK BE NIMBLE'S REAL CANDLE

Provide each child with a copy of the Jack Be Nimble pattern. On the bottom of a sheet of paper, glue a real birthday cake candle. Color and cut out Jack and glue him jumping over the candle.

BAA, BAA, BLACK SHEEP COLOR CARD PATTERN

Enlarge and copy the sheep pattern eleven times. Color each sheep a different color. Directions are found on page 106.

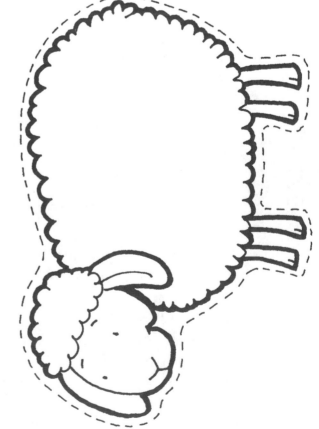

Theme 23: What Grows in the Garden? (Plants and Spring)

	Activity 1	Activity 2	Activity 3	Activity 4
Monday	This week the children are going to talk about planting gardens and spring. **DISCUSSION TOPIC: MAY DAY** May Day is a fun spring celebration. People secretly bring baskets to their neighbors. They knock on the door, leave the basket, then run away.	**MAY DAY HISTORY AND CELEBRATIONS** Complete directions for this activity can be found on page 112.	**MAKE MAY BASKETS** Complete directions for this activity can be found on page 112.	**MAY DAY PARTY** Have a May Day party to celebrate the warm weather and the beginning of spring. A "springy" drink to serve is made by mixing orange juice and strawberries in a blender. It is healthy and tastes as good as a milk shake!
Tuesday	**DISCUSSION TOPIC: THE BIRDS ARE BACK** One of the fun things that the children can observe about spring is that the birds are returning. The birds begin to sing early in the morning.	**LET'S HELP THE BIRDS** The birds are busy building their nests. The children will delight in helping the birds by providing them with some nest construction materials. Fill a mesh net with brightly colored yarn and string and let the children observe the birds taking them away. It is also fun to take a walk and see if you can spot the yarn in nearby nests.	**LEARN THREE BIRDS** The children will learn to identify three birds. Color the bird patterns and cut out. Attach a string to the top of their heads, tie to a small dowel rod, and hang as a bird mobile. Bird patterns and information about the birds can be found on page 113.	**LITTLE BIRD** Quiet, don't say a word. Up in the tree is a little bird. She's building her home, A small little nest. Where she'll lay her eggs And she can rest. She sings a loud, Beautiful song. I hope she stays very long. Quiet, don't say a word. Up in the tree is a little bird.
Wednesday	**SHOW-AND-TELL DAY WEDNESDAY** **DISCUSSION TOPIC: WHAT DO PLANTS NEED?** Find out what the children know about plants. Make a list of their responses. How many of them have gardens at home? What do they grow in their home gardens?	**SEQUENCING PLANT GROWTH CARDS** Have the children each make their own set of plant growth sequencing cards. The reproducible cards can be found on page 114. Color, cut out along the dotted lines, and place in order.	**GARDENING FUN** Gardening can be, So much fun, When you know, What has to be done. Plants need dirt, Water, and sun. And before you know it, A sprout has begun.	**REAL BEAN PLANTS** Let the children grow their own bean plants. Fill styrofoam cups with potting soil. In each cup plant two bean seeds, water, and place in a sunny location. Within 7 to 10 days the seeds will sprout. The children will delight in taking care of their own plants.
Thursday	**DISCUSSION TOPIC: HOW DO SEEDS GROW?** Bring to class a cucumber, an apple, an orange, and some green beans. Cut them open and let the children see and feel the seeds. Discuss how seeds grow into plants.	**LET'S WATCH SEEDS SPROUT** You will need a variety of seeds, paper towels, and resealable plastic bags. Put the seeds between several layers of paper towels and place in plastic bags. Pour in just enough water to soak the paper towels. Staple the paper towels so they are secure in the bags. Attach the bags to a bulletin board that is near sunlight. Soon the seeds will begin to sprout. The children will observe that the roots are reaching toward the water, while the stems reach upward toward the sunlight.		**SPROUTING BULBS** Plant a narcissus bulb in a pot and wait for it to grow. This impressive plant grows quickly. **SPRING CELEBRATION ICE CREAM CAKE** The recipe can be found on page 112. Make the ice cream cake today, but do not serve it until tomorrow.
Friday	**SPECIAL NEWS FRIDAY** **DISCUSSION TOPIC: FLOWERS** Build a florist shop play area and let the children enjoy flower arranging. Ask parents to donate artificial flowers. These flowers can also be used for matching and sorting activities.	**CEREAL MOSAIC FLOWERS** Use the flower pattern on page 112. Fill the inside of the petals and leaves with white glue. Use colorful cereal to create mosaics. **TISSUE PAPER FLOWERS** A flower pattern and complete directions can be found on page 112.	**FLOWER MATCHING** Use artificial flowers for matching activities or create two identical flower card sets using garden catalogs. Coloring books are also an inexpensive resource for creating teacher-made instructional materials.	**SERVE SPRING CELEBRATION ICE CREAM CAKE** While the children are enjoying the special treat, review all the things they have learned this week about spring, planting, and taking care of a garden.

MAY DAY HISTORY AND CELEBRATIONS

Many years ago in England, people were so happy that the cold days of winter were over that they would celebrate the warm weather of spring. The King and Queen would get up early and lead their townspeople in gathering spring flowers. People danced around tall poles that were decorated with the flowers that they collected. The girls of the village all wanted the be the "Queen of the May" but only one lucky girl was chosen.

In the United States, we still think celebrating May Day is fun. Children gather flowers and place them in a basket. The children bring the basket to the home of a neighbor, knock on the door, leave the basket, and then run away. Set up a pole in your classroom, put on some fun music, and let the children dance around the maypole.

MAY BASKETS

To make the basket: Fold a 9" x 12" piece of construction paper in two and staple the sides. Add a handle by stapling a strip of construction paper to the sides.

To make the flowers: Prepare for the children a wide variety of colored construction paper flower shapes. Use the illustration below as a guide. The children can glue the flower shapes on the tops of tongue depressors, and then glue a couple of green construction paper leaves onto each flower.

CELEBRATING SPRING ICE CREAM CAKE

You will need: 1 angel food cake mix; a half-gallon of vanilla ice cream; 2 quarts of different flavored sherbet.

Directions: Grease a 9" x 13" cake pan. Break the cake into small pieces. Alternate between putting the cake, vanilla ice cream, and sherbet into the cake pan. Press gently. Freeze overnight.

TISSUE PAPER FLOWERS

Copy the flower pattern. Cut colored tissue paper into squares. Show the children how to lightly crumple the paper. Dip an edge of a piece of crumpled tissue paper into white glue and press it inside a petal. Keep adding tissue paper until all the flower petals are filled with tissue.

Flower Pattern

LEARN ABOUT THREE BIRDS

CARDINALS
Cardinals are beautiful birds. The male cardinal is bright red. The female cardinal is primarily greenish-gray with red on her wings. These birds love to sing and have beautiful voices. Many years ago people actually kept them as song birds. They eat insects and seeds.

BLUE JAYS
Blue Jays are related to the crow. They have a loud and unpleasant voice. It sounds like they are screaming "thief, thief!" Although they do not sound very nice, they are beautiful to look at. They are a vibrant blue. Blue jays are bullies. They pick on other birds and sometimes try to steal their eggs.

ROBINS
Robins are easy to recognize. They are brown with red stomachs. Robins like to return home after the winter months. They often build their nests in the same place year after year. Robins are good parents. They lay three to six bright blue eggs. Both parents take care of the baby birds.

Robin

Blue Jay   Cardinal

Sequencing Plant Growth Cards

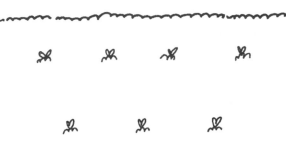

Plants need soil.

Seeds need sunshine.

Plants need water.

Plants need soil, sunshine, and water.

Theme 24: Who Says, "Moo," "Quack," and "Oink?" (The Farm)

	Activity 1	Activity 2	Activity 3	Activity 4
Monday	This week the children are going to talk about life on the farm. Let's make a list of everything we know about farms. Do you know anyone who lives on a farm? Have you ever been to a farm? **DISCUSSION TOPIC: FOOD GROWN ON A FARM** So many foods we eat are grown on a farm.	**CHILDREN'S BOOKS ABOUT THE FARM** Read several books about farms. Leave them out for the children to enjoy during free-time moments. A Children's Literature Reference Guide can be found on pages 158–160.	**FARM STICK PUPPETS** Reproducible farm puppet patterns can be found on page 116. Make a copy of this page for each child. Have the children color, cut out along the dotted lines, and tape the patterns to tongue depressors or craft sticks. Let the children retell some of the farm stories they have heard or have them make up their own stories.	**FARM BULLETIN BOARD** Throughout the week the children will create a farm mural. Cover a bulletin board in light blue paper. Make grass by having the children tear squares of green construction paper. Glue the green paper squares to the bottom of the bulletin board to represent the grass.
Tuesday	**DISCUSSION TOPIC: FOOD THAT COMES FROM ANIMALS** Review the food you discussed yesterday. Today the class will learn about foods that come from animals. *(You may choose to discuss meat, but the activities today only discuss dairy and egg products.)*	**MAKE BUTTER** Butter is fun to make! Every child will need a baby food jar or a container that will not leak. Pour whipping cream and a dash of salt into each jar (1/3 full). Seal tightly and have the children shake the jars. As the butter thickens, pour off the liquid into a large bowl. Serve the butter on bread. Talk about where dairy products come from.	**EGGS!** We learned that dairy products come from cows and goats. Where do eggs come from? Make hard-boiled eggs and serve with the butter and bread. **FARM MURAL** Add a barn and a farm house to your farm mural scene.	**NEWSPAPER SEARCH** Have the children go through grocery advertisements in the newspaper. Cut out all the foods that come from a farm. Cover another bulletin board with paper and let the children fill it with all the food pictures they found in the newspapers.
Wednesday	**SHOW-AND-TELL DAY WEDNESDAY** **DISCUSSION TOPIC: OTHER ANIMALS ON THE FARM** Yesterday the children talked about cows, goats, and chickens. What other animals are found on a farm? What do they do?	**ANIMAL SOUNDS GUESSING GAME** Review all the sounds that farm animals make before playing the game. Have the children take turns making an animal sound and letting the other children guess which animal makes that sound. Children will also enjoy making their own animal sounds tape recording.	**SIX LITTLE DUCKS SONG** The words to the song and patterns can be found on page 117. **FARM MURAL** Add a pond and trees to your farm mural.	**MAKE A WADDLING DUCK** Copy the patterns found on page 119. Color the duck and feet wheel. Attach the wheel with a brass fastener where marked.
Thursday	**DISCUSSION TOPIC: EVEN MORE FARM ANIMALS** During the spring a farm is busy with the births of all the new baby animals. Talk about the names of parent and baby animals: cow-calf, horse-colt, chicken-chick, pig-piglet, sheep-lamb, duck-duckling, cat-kitten, dog-puppy, goose-gosling.	**PARENT AND BABY ANIMALS** Use the reproducible patterns found on pages 118–119 to make a parent and baby animal matching game. Complete directions are found on page 118.	**ANIMAL GUESSING GAMES** Give the children all sorts of clues and see if they can guess which animal you are thinking about. 1. I love the mud and have a curly tail. *(pig)* 2. I am very large and love to eat grass. I can give people all sorts of great food—especially ice cream. *(cow)* 3. People like to ride me. I am large and can help work on the farm. *(horse)* 4. I like to wake people up in the morning. As soon as I see the sun, I let out a loud noise. *(rooster)* 5. I help people stay warm. I am so soft. *(sheep)* Let the children come up with their own clues.	
Friday	**SPECIAL NEWS FRIDAY** **DISCUSSION TOPIC: LET'S PUT IT ALL TOGETHER** Review everything the children have learned about the farm.	**SING "OLD MCDONALD HAD A FARM"** Use the parent and baby animal pictures on pages 118–119 as clues when you sing the song with the children.	**FARM MURAL** Finish the farm mural with animals today. Let the children draw and color their own animals. Help the children cut them out, then add them to the bulletin board. Be sure to take a picture of the mural because it will be adorable!	**ANIMAL CRACKERS** Enjoy your farm unit by letting the children snack on some animal crackers. **Idea 1:** You can also use the crackers in sorting and patterning activities. **Idea 2:** Have the children draw their own farm scene. Glue the animal crackers to the scene.

Farm Stick Puppets

Directions are found on page 115.

| farmer | farmer's wife | farmer's son |

| farmer's daughter | dog | cat |

| cow | horse | pig |

Six Little Ducks

(Let each of the children make their own set of ducks. They can use them to act out the song as they sing it.)

Six little ducks went out to play,
Over the hill and far away.
Mother duck said, "Quack, quack, quack,"
And five little ducks came waddling back.

Five little ducks went out to play,
Over the hill and far away.
Mother duck said, "Quack, quack, quack,"
And four little ducks came waddling back.

Four little ducks went out to play,
Over the hill and far away.
Mother duck said, "Quack, quack, quack,"
And three little ducks came waddling back.

Three little ducks went out to play,
Over the hill and far away.
Mother duck said, "Quack, quack, quack,"
And two little ducks came waddling back.

Two little ducks went out to play,
Over the hill and far away.
Mother duck said, "Quack, quack, quack,"
And one little duck came waddling back.

One little duck went out to play,
Over the hill and far away.
Mother duck said, "Quack, quack, quack,"
And no little ducks came waddling back.

Parent and Baby Animals
Copy, color, cut out along the dotted lines, and laminate for durability.
Shuffle the cards and let the children match the parent animal to it's baby.

Parent and Baby Animals continued. . .

Waddling Duck Patterns

Theme 25: Bugs, Beetles, and Other Creepy Crawly Things (Insects)

	Activity 1	Activity 2	Activity 3	Activity 4
Monday	This week the children are going to learn about insects, butterflies, turtles, frogs, and toads. **DISCUSSION TOPIC: INSECTS THAT CRAWL** Let's begin the week by talking about insects that crawl. Ask the children to name as many insects as they can that crawl.	**ANT FARM** Ants are busy little insects that are a great deal of fun to watch. It is fairly easy to build a classroom ant farm. Complete directions are found on page 121.	**INSECT MATCH** Complete directions for this activity can be found on page 121. **ANTS ON A LOG** Make "ants on a log" as a treat. Spread peanut butter on celery and line raisins along the top.	**THE ANTS GO MARCHING** The well-known song, "The Ants Go Marching" is a fun song to learn during this instructional unit. Try to make up new verses, such as, "The ants go marching one by one, the little one stopped to chew some gum..." Just like real ants, have the children march in a line as they sing the song.
Tuesday	**DISCUSSION TOPIC: INSECTS THAT FLY** Today the children are going to talk about insects that fly. Who can name some flying insects? Does anyone have a favorite insect?	**FIREFLIES** To a child, a firefly is a magical creature. Here is an idea for making fireflies that really glow. Glue three little craft pom-poms together. Add small construction paper wings. Add "glow in the dark" paint to the top of the pom-poms and let dry. Hold the bugs up to a lamp and then turn off the lights. Surprise! The bugs glow!	**LADYBUGS** Children seem to love ladybugs. Make ladybug number cards. The pattern and directions for this activity can be found on page 121.	**BUMBLEBEES** Many children are afraid of bees–and rightly so! Bees are also responsible for providing us with honey. Bring some honey to school and let the children sample it on corn muffins—YUM! On page 122 you will find a bumblebee hive maze. Copy and let the children figure it out!
Wednesday	**SHOW-AND-TELL DAY WEDNESDAY** **DISCUSSION TOPIC: BUTTERFLIES** The children have learned about insects that crawl and fly, now let's talk about butterflies.	**WHERE DO BUTTERFLIES COME FROM?** Teach the children the life cycle of a butterfly. Reproducible life cycle cards can be found on page 123.	**MATCHING WINGS** Cut out a pair of butterfly wings. Fold in two. Put drops of paint on one wing. Fold the other wing over and press. Open and both wings should look identical. Glue on a pipe cleaner for an antennae.	**COLOR A REAL BUTTERFLY** On page 123 you will find a realistic illustration of a butterfly. Make a copy for each of the children. Provide crayons, colored pencils, and markers and allow the children to color the butterfly anyway they want to!
Thursday	**DISCUSSION TOPIC: TURTLES** Children are always fascinated with turtles. They are intriguing to watch and fun to learn about. Talk about the turtles that we find in our ponds and compare them with the great sea turtles.	**PAPER PLATE TURTLES** For this activity, purchase the sturdy paper plates. Cut out five green ovals for each child. These will become the head and four feet. Glue to the bottom of the plate. Paint the back of the paper plate green. Let dry. Glue small torn paper on top of the green paint. This will give the turtle a realistic "shell" look.	**CATCH AND RELEASE CAN** All the children will need an oatmeal container. Cut a window in one side and tape a screen or netting over the window. Explain to the children that this is only for catching bugs and other small creatures to look at. They must let them go. Small animals and bugs are not meant to be pets.	**NATURE WALK** Take the children on a walk outside. Look for insects, butterflies, and turtles! See if they can find anything to put in their "Catch and Release Cans." Be sure to let the critters go when you are done looking at them!
Friday	**SPECIAL NEWS FRIDAY** **DISCUSSION TOPIC: FROGS AND TOADS** Although frogs and toads have different names, in reality they are both types of frogs.	**LIFE CYCLE OF A FROG** Show the children pictures of the life cycle of a frog. Their life cycle is amazing. The transformation from egg to tadpole and then frog is really a miracle to watch. There are scientific companies that you can contact to purchase frog eggs for your classroom. This is a truly exciting experience.	**FROG AND TOAD PUZZLES** Find each of the body parts to put together a frog and a toad. Patterns and complete directions are found on page 124.	**FROG AND TOAD ARE FRIENDS** Read the book, *Frog and Toad are Friends,* by Arnold Lobel.

ANT FARM

Here are some easy directions for making your own classroom ant farm. You will need a large glass gallon jar, dirt, cotton, cheesecloth, and dark paper. Fill the jar halfway with dirt. Now go outside and find an active ant hill. With a shovel, carefully dig down and scoop the hill out of the ground and put it in the jar. Place some cotton on top and pour a small amount of water on it every other day for the ants to drink.

At first, cover the jar with dark paper so the ants become accustomed to their new surroundings and begin to dig tunnels. Punch holes in the lid so the ants have air and cover with cheesecloth. Not only will the ants need water, but you need to provide them food. Ants will like sugar water, honey, and bread crumbs.

INSECT MATCH

This is a wonderful idea for making a variety of teaching materials. The idea is to be able to match two identical objects. The children will be matching insects, but this project can be adapted for colors, shapes, numbers, and any number of objects to match a thematic teaching unit.

You will need: Two clean milk cartons *(whipping cream and half & half cartons also work well);* clear contact paper; two sets of identical insect stickers or pictures; a brass fastener; and scissors.

Directions: Cut the triangular tops off the cartons. Poke a hole in the center of the bottom of each carton. Attach the cartons, bottom to bottom, with the brad. The cartons will turn easily. Choose four insect stickers and place one on each of the four sides of the left carton. Repeat on the right side of the carton. The children will spin the cartons to match the identical stickers.

LADYBUG NUMBER MATCHING

Copy the ladybug pattern for as many numerals as your classroom of children are ready to learn. Notice the dotted lines between the wings. On one wing print the numeral. On the other wing, place the corresponding number of dots. Let the children enjoy matching the ladybugs.

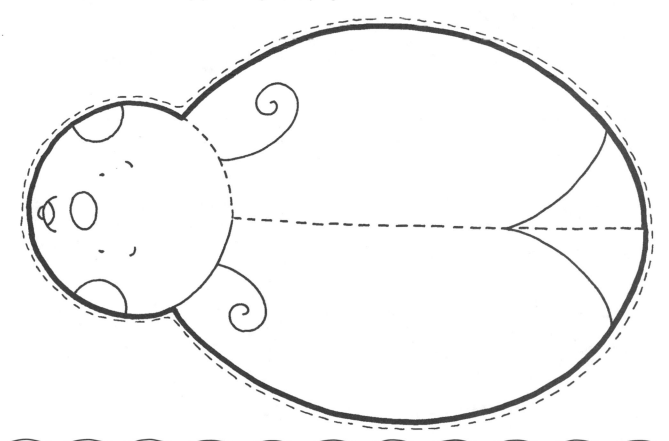

Bumblebee Hive Maze

Help the worker bee find his way in to see the Queen Bee.

A Realistic Butterfly

Life Cycle of a Butterfly

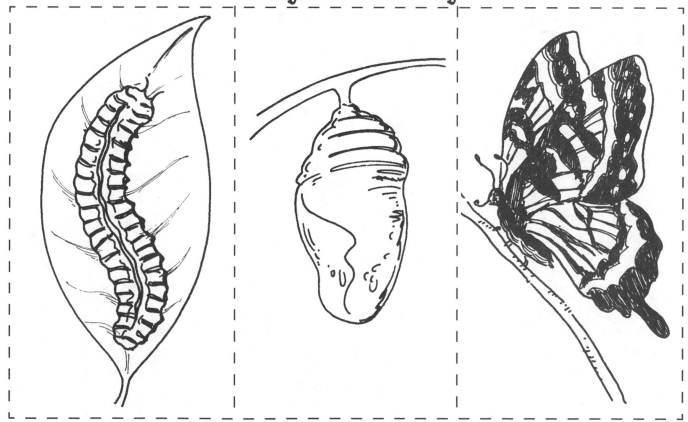

Frog and Toad Puzzles

Cut out each of the pieces and assemble into a frog and a toad.
Glue onto a piece of paper and then color. Frog should be green and toad should be brown.

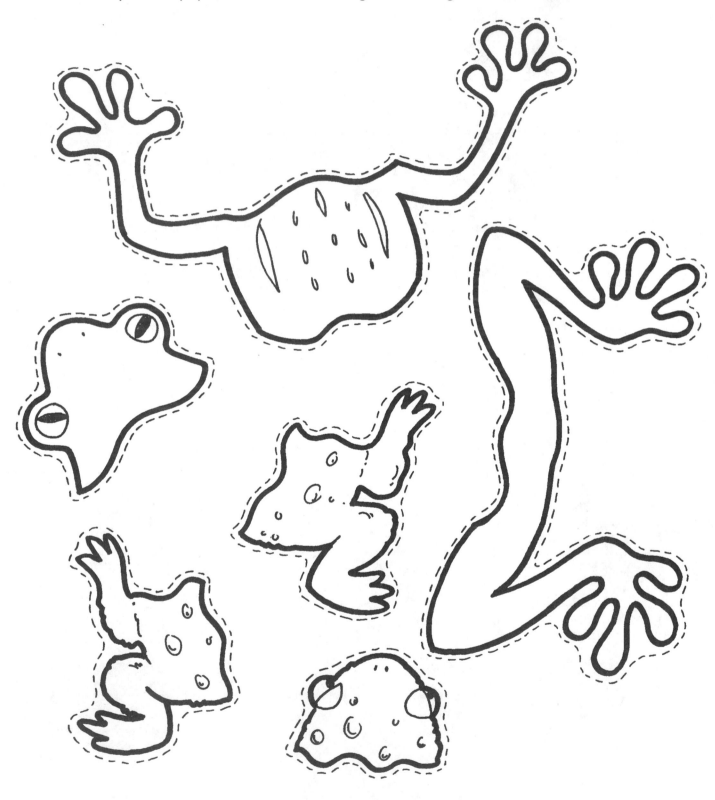

Theme 26: Early Childhood Olympics (Staying Fit)

	Activity 1	Activity 2	Activity 3	Activity 4
Monday	This week the children are going to prepare for their own Olympics Day. Find out what the children already know about the Olympics. Discuss ways to build strong bodies. **DISCUSSION TOPIC: LEARN ABOUT THE OLYMPICS** Has anyone ever seen the Olympics on TV? Discuss the history of the Olympics.	**THE OLYMPIC MOTTO** In Latin, the motto is, "Citius, Altius, Fortius," which means "swifter, higher, stronger." These are the goals for the athletes. Have the children come up with a motto for their Olympics. A reproducible motto can be found on page 126.	**THE OLYMPIC FLAME** The Olympic flame is lit by the Olympic torch. After the torch is lit it is carried by thousands of people, through many countries, until it reaches the stadium where the Olympics will take place. Make an Olympic flame and torch. Complete directions are found on page 127.	**OLYMPIC DAY INVITATIONS** Complete directions for making Olympic Day torch invitations can be found on page 127. **THE OLYMPIC SYMBOL** The symbol contains five circles linked together. It is a reminder of good sportsmanship. The ring has five colors: blue, yellow, black, green, and red. A reproducible Olympic symbol is on page 127 for the children to color.
Tuesday	**DISCUSSION TOPIC: WHY IS EXERCISE IMPORTANT?** Ask the children what they think the word "exercise" means. Why is it important? Discuss how hard the Olympic athletes exercise and practice.	**DAILY EXERCISE PLAN** Explain to the children that to prepare for their Olympics Day, they will have to exercise and practice everyday just like the Olympic athletes. Begin your exercising with this warm-up rhyme: **"Touch your shoe–1, 2. Jump with me–1, 2, 3. Jump some more–1, 2, 3, 4. Arms up high–1, 2, 3, 4, and 5."** Then decide on a set exercise routine, which is more fun when performed to music. *Here are some ideas:* 10–jumping jacks; 10–toe-touches; 10–sit-ups; 5–push-ups; and, 10 arm stretches. Dancing to music is great exercise too! End your exercise routine with the above rhyme.		**WHO IS EXERCISING?** Create an exercise bulletin board. Have the children cut out pictures from magazines and newspapers of people who are exercising, and pictures of exercise equipment. Display the pictures on the bulletin board.
Wednesday	SHOW-AND-TELL DAY WEDNESDAY **DISCUSSION TOPIC: PLANNING THE EVENTS** Depending on the size of your class, you will have to decide if the children can participate in all of the events or choose just a few. During practice, give the children the opportunity to try all six events.	**PAIRS JUMPING** This event is a sack race. Burlap bags can often be located at grocery stores or can easily be made. Two children get into one bag and hop to the finish line. You can either have this event as a group race or the children can take turns individually.	**DISCUS THROWING** Use sturdy paper plates as frisbees. Each child should have their own. Decorate the plates before the event.	**LONG JUMP** This event should be performed on grass or in the sand for safety. Do not hold this event on pavement or cement. Place a tape measure on the ground to measure how far the children jump.
Thursday	**DISCUSSION TOPIC: THE GRAND ENTRANCE OF COUNTRIES** Today the children will continue learning the events, but will also learn how to enter with the Olympic torch. Teach the children how to line up single file and then pass the torch to each other. Make sure all the children have an opportunity to hold and pass the torch.	**WATER RELAYS** This is messy and tons of fun. Have the children form four lines. At the beginning of each line is a bowl of water and four soup spoons. At the end of the line is an empty bowl. The children run a relay, taking a spoonful of water and walking carefully to the other bowl and pouring it in. The team that transfers the most water wins.	**NERF™ BALL SHOT PUT** Using a soft Nerf™ ball, teach the children how to throw a shot put. Let the children take turns and measure how far the Nerf™ ball was shot putted.	**JAVELIN THROWING** Use a wrapping paper cardboard tube for this event. Teach the children how to throw the javelin properly. Mark where the javelin first touches down.
Friday	SPECIAL NEWS FRIDAY **DISCUSSION TOPIC: PREPARATION FOR OLYMPICS DAY** Set up the events in 6 stations. Have a parent volunteer at each station. Let the children rotate through all the events.	**SET-UP** Set up a water table with paper cups, and also construct a platform for the medal ceremony. Decorate with Olympic symbols, streamers, and the motto of the Olympics *(found on page 126)*. Prepare refreshments to be served after the medal ceremony. Lemonade and cookies would be nice.	**AN OLYMPIC MEDAL AND MOTTO** Make an Olympic medal for each child. Tie it on a ribbon so it can be presented at the Olympics ceremony and worn home. (Reproducible medal pattern can be found on page 126.)	**OLYMPICS DAY** It is the big day! At the conclusion of the day have a medals ceremony. Everyone gets a medal. One at a time, the children can stand on the platform, be presented with their Olympics Day medal, and have their pictures taken.

An Olympic Medal

THIS MEDAL
IS AWARDED TO:

_____

⊨ FOR: ⊨

_____

_____

 THE OLYMPIC MOTTO

"CITIUS, ALTIUS,  FORTIUS"

MEANS:

"SWIFTER, HIGHER, STRONGER."

OLYMPIC FLAME AND TORCH

Make a classroom Olympic flame by filling a large bowl with red, orange, and gold tissue paper. Place the bowl on top of a stool that has been decorated with streamers. Make a classroom torch from a paper towel tube. Stuff the top of the tube with red, orange, and gold tissue paper.

```
┌ ─ ─ ─ ─ ─ ─ ─ ─ ─ ┐
│   YOUR ARE INVITED TO OUR   │
│     SCHOOL OLYMPICS DAY      │
│                              │
│  DATE: _____     │
│                              │
│  TIME: _____     │
│                              │
│  PLACE: _____     │
└ ─ ─ ─ ─ ─ ─ ─ ─ ─ ┘
```

OLYMPIC DAY INVITATIONS

The finished invitations will look similar to the classroom torch. Prepare ahead of time, and have a copy for each child, a 2" x 3" invitation. It should include all the important information that the parents will need: time, place, and date. Use the pattern to the left.

Give each child a brown piece of construction paper. Lay it flat and glue red, orange, and gold tissue paper to the top edge. Let the glue dry. Roll the paper into a cylinder and tape. Glue the invitation to the cylinder. The children can bring it home to invite their parents and other family members, and explain what they have learned about the Olympics

The Olympic Symbol

Theme 27: Growl! Roar! (Jungle Animals)

	Activity 1	Activity 2	Activity 3	Activity 4
Monday	This week the children are going to learn about wild jungle animals. Talk about how they can see them in the zoo, but that they are happier in their natural habitat. **DISCUSSION TOPIC: LIONS AND ELEPHANTS** Be sure to read the factual information on pages 129–131 before introducing any of the animals.	**THE KING OF THE BEASTS** Teach the children some factual information about the lion (page 129). Be sure to have books available for the children to look at. Let the children create a paper plate lion puppet. Glue yarn around the edge of a paper plate and draw a face. As a special touch make the lion a crown.	**THE HUGE ELEPHANT** Elephants are incredible animals. Share the factual information about elephants found on page 129.	**MY WILD ANIMAL BOOK** Every day the children will be adding at least two pages to their Wild Animal Books, found on pages 129–131. Today have the children color the cover and complete pages 2 (lion) and 3 (elephant). Review what the children have learned about the animals.
Tuesday	**DISCUSSION TOPIC: ZEBRAS AND GIRAFFES** The animals we are going to learn about today–zebras and giraffes–are two of the most unusual and beautiful. Both have incredible markings. Ask the children to describe what these animals look like before you show them any pictures.	**ZEBRA STRIPES** The most amazing feature about a zebra is its beautiful black-and-white stripes. Give each child the outline shape of a horse. With black crayons let the children add their own stripe patterns. This is also fun when the horse outline is on black paper and the children add white stripes with chalk.	**THE TALLEST GIRAFFE** Make up a fun story about all the things you could do if we had necks that were six feet long. What could you reach that you cannot reach now? This would be a tall tale. Giraffes have spots. Provide the children with an outline of a giraffe. Paint gold and let dry. Add spots by putting a finger in brown paint and finger printing the spots.	**MY WILD ANIMAL BOOK CONTINUED...** Today the children should complete pages 4 (zebra) and 5 (giraffe) in their Wild Animal Books. Reproducible pages found on pages 129–130.
Wednesday	**SHOW-AND-TELL DAY WEDNESDAY** **DISCUSSION TOPIC: OSTRICH AND CHIMPANZEE** Today the children will learn about two more remarkable animals. Review the four the children have learned about so far. Make a list of what makes them the same and different.	**THE OSTRICH** The other animals we have learned about so far were covered in fur. What is covering the ostrich? Bring in some different textures for the children to touch. Make texture squares by using a variety of fabrics and materials that can be found at any fabric store: feathers, suede, faux fur, and vinyl.	**CHIMPANZEES** Chimpanzees have been taught sign language. Teach the children several signs and encourage them to use those signs throughout the day: yes, no, please, thank you, eat, drink, toilet, play. As a fun treat while you are learning about chimps, make frozen bananas. Place on a stick, roll in crushed nuts or chocolate, and freeze.	**MY WILD ANIMAL BOOK CONTINUED...** Today the children should complete pages 6 (ostrich) and 7 (chimpanzee) in their Wild Animal Books. Reproducible page found on page 130.
Thursday	**DISCUSSION TOPIC: HIPPOPOTAMUS AND CROCODILE** The animals we will learn about today both love the water. They both appear lazy during the day but are busy eating in the evening.	**HIPPOPOTAMUS** Hippos spend most of the day just swimming and floating in the water. Make a floating hippo. Using clay, mold the shape of a hippo. Clay will float.	**CROCODILE** Use a tape measure and mark off 25 feet. The children will be amazed to see how long 25 feet is and to learn that the very largest crocodiles can actually reach this length. Have the children lie down along this line. How many children will it take to be as long as the crocodile?	**MY WILD ANIMAL BOOK CONTINUED...** Today the children should complete pages 8 (hippopotamus) and 9 (crocodile) in their Wild Animal Books. Reproducible pages found on pages 130–131.
Friday	**SPECIAL NEWS FRIDAY** **DISCUSSION TOPIC: RHINOCEROS AND PYTHON** Pythons and rhinos both prefer to live alone. Rhinos are unpredictable and aggressive, while pythons can be calm and are not aggressive unless they are hungry.	**RHINOCEROS** Rhinos have very poor eyesight and rely on their sense of smell. A sudden new smell can make them charge. Create small jars of "odors." Can the children guess the "smell?" Here are some good things to use: lemons, cocoa, vinegar, perfume, soup, and apple juice.	**PYTHONS** Make a classroom python. Have the children look at pictures of snakes. Study the patterns. Are there stripes? Spots? Give each child a 4" x 6" index card. Have them color the card with snake patterns. Attach all the cards together with brass fasteners. The giant snake will slither.	**MY WILD ANIMAL BOOK CONTINUED...** Today the children should complete pages 10 (rhinoceros) and 11 (python), and sign their names on page 12, as an animal expert (see page 131). **MATCHING ANIMAL PARTS** Complete directions and patterns can be found on pages 132–133.

Wild Animal Book

My **Wild** Animal Book

-1-

Lion

The lion was named the "King of the Beasts," because he is so strong and so fierce. A lion can grow from 7 to 11 feet long and weigh up to 500 pounds. Lions sleep during the day and hunt at night. Only male lions have manes and they start to grow when they are 3 years old.

-2-

Elephant

The elephant is the world's largest land animal. They can grow up to 11 feet tall and weigh up to 14,000 pounds. They use their huge ears as fans. An elephant will spend 16 hours a day eating!

-3-

Zebra

The zebra looks like a striped horse. Zebras might look like horses but they are stubborn and not as gentle as horses. You cannot ride a zebra. Their stripes help them hide in the tall grasses.

-4-

Wild Animal Book

Giraffe

The giraffe is the tallest animal in the world. It can grow up to 18 feet tall and can weigh 4,000 pounds. It's neck can be 6 feet long. Giraffes can see in all directions without moving their heads. They like to eat fruit and leaves.

-5-

Ostrich

The ostrich is the world's largest bird. They can grow to be 8 feet tall and weigh between 200 and 300 pounds. Now that is a big bird! They have great eyesight and can see for several miles. An ostrich will eat anything!

-6-

Chimpanzee

The chimpanzee is the smartest of all the apes. They can grow to 5 feet tall and weigh up to 180 pounds. They can make simple tools and use sticks as toys. Chimpanzees can make facial expressions that show if they are happy, sad, or angry. They can also learn sign language.

-7-

Hippopotamus

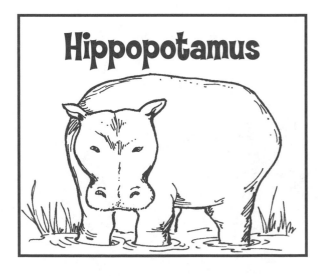

The hippopotamus is the second largest land animal. They are related to the hog family and actually look like a pig. The common hippo can grow to 12 feet in length and weigh up to 8,000 pounds. Hippos love the water. Most hippo babies can swim before they can walk on land.

-8-

Wild Animal Book

Crocodile

The crocodile is a very dangerous animal. They are green and have scale-like skin. The largest of the crocodiles can grow to be 25 feet long. They like warm weather. They spend the day laying in the sun and they spend their nights hunting for food. Mother crocodiles carry their babies in their mouths.

-9-

Rhinoceros

The rhinoceros is a huge animal. It can weigh up to 2 tons and grow as long as 12 feet. The rhino is actually a relative of the horse. It can even run as fast as a horse. The rhino is easily identified by its horns, which are made from claw and hair materials.

-10-

Python

The python is a gigantic snake. It's skin is covered with smooth, dry scales. Snakes always look like they are awake. Their eyes are always open because they do not have any eyelids. Snakes do not have ears but they can hear low sounds and they smell with their tongues.

-11-

This certificate is proudly presented to "Wild Animal Expert"

_____

Congratulations!
You have learned so much about wild animals!

signed by _____

-12-

Matching Animal Parts

The patterns for this activity are found on this page and page 133. Copy, color, and cut out. The children can match the correct head to the body. For some silly fun, you can mismatch the heads and bodies and make some really funny looking wild animals.

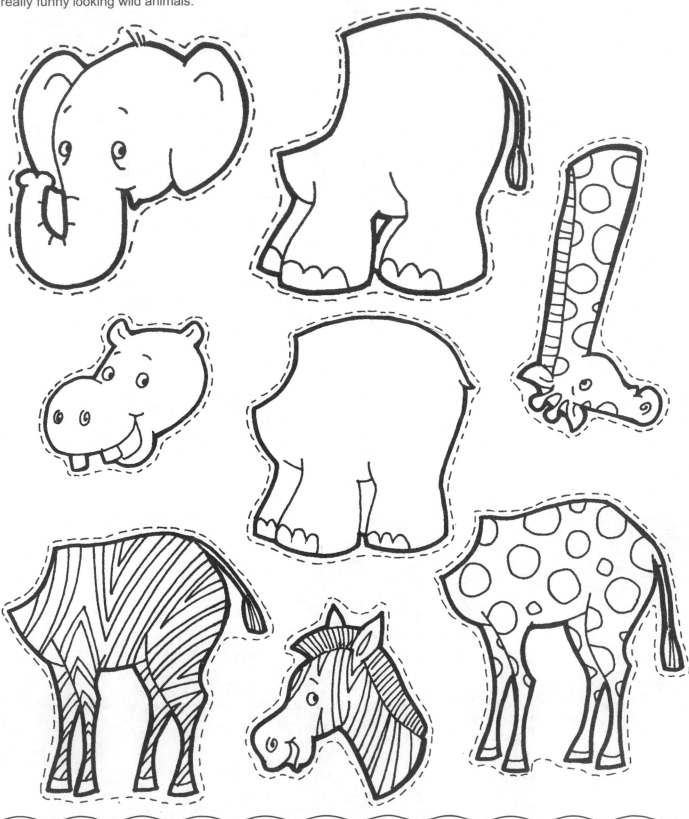

Matching Animal Parts Continued...

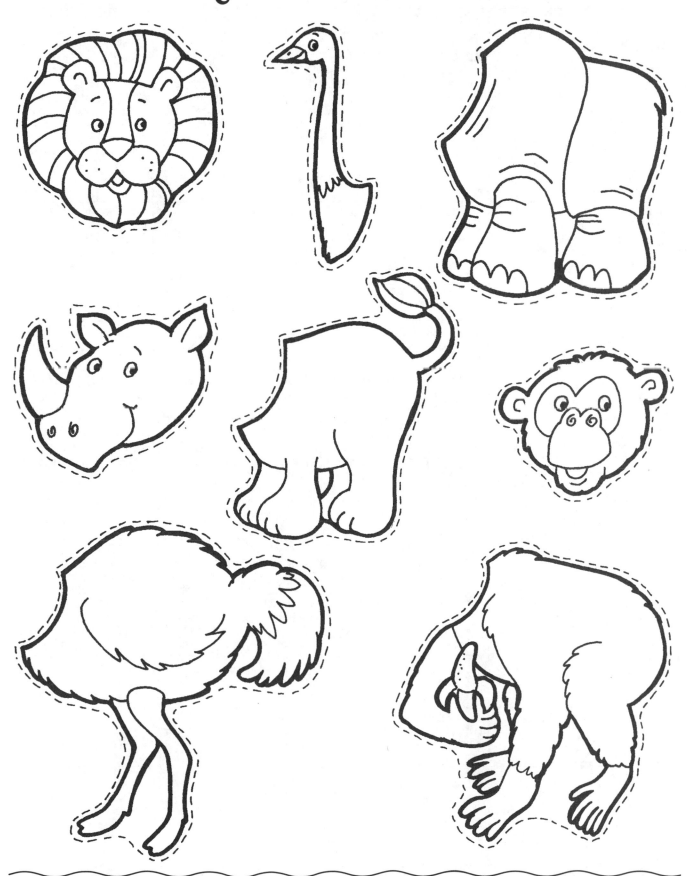

Theme 28: We are Proud of Our Country (Citizenship/Patriotism)

	Activity 1	Activity 2	Activity 3	Activity 4
Monday	This week the children are going to discuss what it means to be a good citizen and learn more about their country. This theme has been written so that it is appropriate for the **UNITED STATES** and for **CANADA**. **DISCUSSION TOPIC: PRESIDENT/PRIME MINISTER** What are some of the responsibilities of the leader?	**PRESIDENT/PRIME MINISTER PHOTOGRAPHS** Show the children photographs of the President/Prime Minister. Have the children learn his name. Ask the children if they know how he became the leader.	**WE VOTE FOR OUR LEADERS** Discuss voting with the children. This is how the people decide who they want as their leaders. It is fair and democratic. Vote on things throughout the week. Vote for which book is read at story time; vote for who gets to be line leader; vote for what game the children will play outside.	**IF I WERE PRESIDENT/ PRIME MINISTER** Use the reproducible activity found on page 135. Have the children draw and color their pictures inside the frames. Have them dictate to you a statement about what they would do if they were in charge of the country.
Tuesday	**DISCUSSION TOPIC: SYMBOLS OF OUR COUNTRY** Explain to the children the concept of symbols. Show the children pictures of some symbols, places, and things that are important to their country.	**FLAGS** Show the children their country's flag. (Information about the flags is found on pages 136 and 137.) Discuss the history of their flag. Make a flag using construction paper. **DESIGN A CLASSROOM FLAG** Discuss this and choose meaningful symbols for your flag.	**ANIMAL NATIONAL SYMBOLS** Discuss the American bald eagle or the Canadian beaver. (Factual information is found on page 136 and 137.) Read the children information about the real animals. Talk about why these animals are important to their country. What animal would you choose as a national symbol?	**I AM PROUD TO BE A CANADIAN OR AN AMERICAN** Use the reproducible four-page fold books, found on pages 136 and 137. **LEARN YOUR COUNTRY'S NATIONAL ANTHEM** The correct words can be found on pages 136 and 137.
Wednesday	**SHOW-AND-TELL DAY WEDNESDAY** **DISCUSSION TOPIC: LET'S BE GOOD CITIZENS** The children have learned something about their country's leader and about some of their country's symbols. Today we are going to learn about being good citizens.	**WHAT IS A GOOD CITIZEN?** Explain to the children that to be a citizen means that you are a member of a group. The children are citizens of their classroom, families, neighborhoods, and country. The first rule of being a good citizen is understanding that we need rules and should obey them. Write a list of classroom rules. What happens when rules are broken?	**EVEN ADULTS FOLLOW RULES** We made a list and know the rules we have to follow as children in this classroom. Even adults have to follow rules. What are some rules that adults follow? What happens when some of the rules are broken? (People can sometimes go to jail.)	**GOOD CITIZEN COUPONS** Reproduce and have on hand many good citizen coupons. (The coupon pattern is found on page 138.) When you catch the children being responsible, respectful, and caring for their environment, give them a coupon. Let the children exchange their coupons on Friday for stickers to take home.
Thursday	**DISCUSSION TOPIC: LEARNING MORE ABOUT CITIZENSHIP** There are many things that we can do to be good citizens. We are going to learn more about them today.	**HOW TO BE A GOOD CITIZEN** We have already learned that, to be a good citizen, we need to follow the rules. Another way to be a good citizen is to be helpful in your home; classroom; neighborhood; and, country. Make pennants that show ways the children can be helpful: do not litter; be kind; be careful with school property.	**A GOOD CITIZENSHIP SCHOOL PROJECT** Look around your school and plan a project that even the youngest children can perform. For instance, purchase a garbage can for the playground and have the children paint it. This is a practical object that will look adorable and help keep their playground clean.	**FIREWORKS CELEBRATION** Many communities have fireworks displays to celebrate something historically important. Create a bulletin board firework display. Cover the bulletin board with black paper. Give each child a piece of black construction paper. Make a white glue design. Sprinkle glitter in a variety of colors on the wet glue.
Friday	**SPECIAL NEWS FRIDAY** **DISCUSSION TOPIC: PUTTING IT ALL TOGETHER** Today will be a busy day. We are going to talk about why we have a great country and why we have a great classroom!	**TRAVEL POSTERS** Let's pretend that we work for a travel agency. We need to make some posters advertising why people from other countries should come and visit our country. **WHERE I LIVE IS GREAT BECAUSE...** Finish this statement, "Where I live is great because..."	**CLASSROOM PLEDGE** As a group, write a classroom pledge. Display it in your room. **MY CLASSROOM IS GREAT BECAUSE...** Finish this statement: "My classroom is great because..."	**A MELTING POT** The United States and Canada are both rich in diversity, with many people from many different countries and cultures. Have the children cut out pictures of different people from old magazines and catalogs. Display all the people on a bulletin board.

If I Were President or Prime Minister

Color your picture. Write or dictate a statement about what you would do if you were in charge of the country.

If I were the leader of our country, I would. . .

_____

_____

_____

Cut along the dotted lines and fold along the solid lines.

-3-
Canada's national flag features the maple leaf, the country's symbol. The red and white flag was decided upon in 1964.

The Canadian Flag

-2-
The beaver became an official National Canadian Symbol in 1975. The beaver has been put on coats of arms, money, and stamps.

The Beaver

"O Canada!"

O Canada!
Our home and native land!
True patriot love in all thy sons command.

With glowing hearts we see thee rise,
The True North strong and free!

From far and wide,
O Canada, we stand on guard for thee.

God keep our land glorious and free!
O Canada, we stand on guard for thee.

O Canada, we stand on guard for thee.

-4-

I Am Proud To Be A Canadian!
This is why:

_____

_____

_____

-1-

Cut along the dotted lines and fold along the solid lines.

-3-

The American flag has 13 stripes for the original 13 colonies and 50 stars for each of the 50 states. The color red stands for hardiness and courage. The color blue stands for justice and perseverance, and the color white stands for purity.

The America Flag

-2-

The bald eagle became an American National Symbol in 1782. It was chosen because it is associated with freedom and courage.

The Bald Eagle

THE STAR-SPANGLED BANNER

Oh say, can you see,
By the dawn's early light,
What so proudly we hailed
At the twilight's last gleaming?
Whose broad stripes and bright stars,
Through the perilous fight,
O'er the ramparts we watched,
Were so gallantly streaming?
And the rockets' red glare,
The bombs bursting in air,
Gave proof through the night
That our flag was still there.
O say, does that star-spangled
Banner yet wave
O'er the land of the free
And the home of the brave?

-4-

I Am Proud To Be An American! This is why:

_____

_____

_____

-1-

Good Citizen Coupons

Today I was a good citizen: I was HELPFUL at school today.

Today I was a good citizen: I was RESPECTFUL at school today.

Today I was a good citizen: I was CONSIDERATE at school today.

Today I was a good citizen: I was A GOOD LISTENER at school today.

Theme 29: Furry Family Members (Pets)

	Activity 1	Activity 2	Activity 3	Activity 4
Monday	This week the children are going to learn about taking care of pets. Try to arrange a field trip to a pet store or veterinary hospital. **DISCUSSION TOPICS: PREPARING FOR THE WEEK.** This is a favorite theme for young children. Talk about who has pets. Send home the parent letter found on page 140.	**WHO HAS A PET OR PETS?** Go around the room and ask the children if they have any pets. Make a list of all the different types of pets and their names. If a child does not have a pet, ask the child if there are any other family members who have a pet, such as an aunt, cousins, grandparents or even a neighbor. Save this information.	**WHAT DO PETS NEED?** Complete directions for this activity can be found on page 140.	**THIS IS WHAT PETS NEED** On pages 141–142 you will find a reproducible book about caring for animals. Copy one for each child in your class.
Tuesday	**DISCUSSION TOPIC: DOGS** Today the children are going to talk about dogs. How many different breeds of dogs can they name? Let's look at our bar graph. How many children in this class have dogs?	**LIST OF PETS** Use the list of pet types and pet names that you wrote down yesterday. Count all the animals and turn it into a bar graph. How many dogs? How many cats? How many hamsters? How many fish? Make a column for each type of animal.	**BOOKS ABOUT DOGS** Read some books about dogs. Can the children name some famous dogs? *(Snoopy, Lassie, 101 Dalmations)* Here are some fun dog facts: Dalmations are pure white when they are born and get spots later. Puppies are born without teeth. At 4 weeks they begin to get 28 teeth. There are more than 150 different breeds of purebred dogs.	**PUPPY PUPPETS** Provide each child with a paper plate. Let the child decide what color dog he would like. Paint the paper plate that color. Cut ears for the dog: floppy ears, pointed ears, or large ears. Add construction paper eyes, nose and mouth.
Wednesday	**SHOW-AND-TELL DAY WEDNESDAY** **DISCUSSION TOPIC: FIELD TRIP** Plan a field trip to a pet store or veterinary clinic. Sometimes a veterinarian is willing to come to a school and give a presentation.	**MOTHER CAT AND THE KITTENS** Choose one child to be a mother or father cat. The parent cat then covers its eyes. Another two children are chosen to be kittens. The kittens hide and quietly meow. The parent cat must find the lost kittens. Make sure all the children have a turn.	**LEARN THE RHYME "THE THREE LITTLE KITTENS"** Have the children memorize the rhyme. Let the children dramatize the rhyme. Choose three children to be the kittens and use real mittens. Put one mitten on each child and hide the other three. Let all the children search for the mittens and match them to the correct child.	**CLASSROOM PET** Find a stuffed animal and turn it into the official classroom pet. The pet gets to go home on the weekends with one of the children. The children are to take care of the toy pet. On Monday, the child tells the class all the things the pet did while at the child's home. *(See page 143 for complete directions and the note to parents.)*
Thursday	**DISCUSSION TOPICS:** Dogs and cats are probably the most common types of pets, but there are many other types of pets: hamsters, chinchillas, rabbits, turtles, fish, ferrets, horses, snakes, and lizards.	**LITTLE BUNNIES** Give each child an outline of a bunny. Let the children fill the inside of the bunny shape by gluing on cotton or quilt batting. Add a nose and eyes made from construction paper.	**WHERE DO YOU LIVE?** Animals live in all sorts of different homes. Make a list of animals and the types of homes they should have. For example: fish need fish bowls or aquariums; hamsters need cages.	**BIRDS** Many children have birds as pets. Let each child make their own bird. Glue a small circle and a large circle together. Glue on some feathers *(purchased at a craft store)*, and add wiggly eyes. Draw a picture of a nest on a piece of paper and glue the bird on the nest.
Friday	**SPECIAL NEWS FRIDAY** **Discussion Topics:** Fish also make interesting pets.	**GO FISHING** Make a fishing pole from a dowel rod. Attach a string with a magnet tied to the end. Make many fish cut outs and put a paper clip on each fish. Print numbers, colors, alphabet letters, or shapes on the fish. Let the children fish and then describe what they have caught. *(Fish pattern on page 140.)*	**I HAVE A PET** *(Sung to the tune of "I'm a Little Teapot.")* I have a little pet, Who's lots of fun. When I call him, He always comes. We run outside, And he chases me. I love him and he loves me!	**ANIMALS AT SCHOOL!** Today is the day when some of the parents have volunteered to bring the family pet to school. Let each child have a turn telling about their pet and walking it around the classroom.

WE ARE LEARNING ABOUT TAKING CARE OF PETS

Dear Parents,

This week the children are learning about pets. We would like to conclude this weekly unit by having as many of the children's pets as possible come and visit our classroom. The pets will need you to bring them and stay with them while they are at school. Please arrive at:_____.

The children will love to show off their animal family members, and they will impress you with how much they have learned about caring for animals.

Thank You,

- -

WHAT DO PETS NEED?

Have a discussion with the children about everything that pets need. It is a huge responsibility to take care of an animal. Here are some questions that you can ask the children.

- Who has a pet?
- Where does your pet sleep?
- Who feeds your pet?
- What does your pet eat?
- Who makes sure that your pet has water?
- Who takes your pet to the veterinarian when it is sick?
- Who plays with your pet?
- What does your pet like to play with?
- What games does your pet play?
- Who walks your pet?
- Who cleans up after your pet?

FISH PATTERN

WHAT DO PETS NEED?

-1-

PETS NEED FOOD AND WATER.

-2-

PETS NEED REST AND A PLACE TO SLEEP.

-3-

PETS NEED TO LEARN MANNERS AND HOW TO BEHAVE.

-4-

PETS NEED TO BE CLEAN AND HAVE GOOD CARE.

-5-

PETS NEED TO PLAY AND BE LOVED!

-6-

OUR SPECIAL CLASSROOM PET

Dear Parents,

Our class is beginning a special project. We now have a classroom pet. Oh, don't worry – it is not a real animal. It is a stuffed _____!

We are all going to take turns bringing it home for the weekend. And this weekend is your child's turn!

Our pet's name is _____. It is your child's responsibility this weekend to take good care of the classroom pet and include him in your family activities.

On Monday, when your child and our pet return to school, your child will be asked to give a brief "share and tell" presentation about how the weekend went. What were some of the activities that the pet participated in? Did the pet get to go anywhere? Help your child write down some ideas. The ideas that you write down will help me guide their presentation about the weekend.

Thank you so much!
Your Child's Teacher

- -

I WENT TO _____'S HOUSE.
THIS IS WHAT I DID WHEN I WAS THERE.

_____

_____

_____

_____

_____

_____

Theme 30: Read me A Story (Early Literacy Skills)

	Activity 1	Activity 2	Activity 3	Activity 4
Monday	This week is called "Read Me a Story." The children are going to listen to some wonderful stories and learn about the people who wrote them. **DISCUSSION TOPIC: DR. SEUSS** Our first author is Dr. Seuss. His books are often the first ones that a child learns to read.	**ABOUT DR. SEUSS** Dr. Suess' real name was Theodor Seuss Geisel. The fun thing to know about Dr. Seuss is that he had trouble drawing. A teacher once even told him to give it up. When he tried to draw, it just always ended up looking funny. The same thing happened with his writing–when he couldn't find the right word, he would just make up a new one. Our lesson from Dr. Seuss is not to give up. Read *Dr. Seuss's ABC Book*. Look at all the funny animals and characters. Have the children make their own classroom ABC book. Assign each child a letter and help them think of something that starts with that letter. Each child will illustrate their page and dictate a silly sentence about the picture. Bind together for a classroom book. Share the whole book with the class. There will be many giggles!		**ONE FISH, TWO FISH** Another great first book for children is *One Fish, Two Fish*. Use the reproducible activity about opposites, found on page 145.
Tuesday	**DISCUSSION TOPIC: ARNOLD LOBEL** Arnold Lobel has written many incredible children's stories and was a remarkable man.	**ABOUT ARNOLD LOBEL** Arnold Lobel was a very kind man, a wonderful storyteller, and a great man who made everyone happy. As a child, he was smaller and not as strong as most of the other children. Because of this, the school bullies teased him. Arnold was very clever–to protect himself he would tell stories and make all the children laugh. This was the beginning of his storytelling skills. Arnold loved nursery rhymes. As a writer, he rewrote some of them which showed how kind he was. The three-blind mice ran faster than the farmer's wife, so she couldn't cut off their tails. His most popular books are about Frog and Toad. They are best friends.		**READ, *FROG AND TOAD TOGETHER*** In the book *Frog and Toad Together,* there is a story called *Giants and Dragons*. Frog and Toad try to be brave. Read their adventure and then draw a picture of your favorite part of the story. ***THE LIST*** Complete directions can be found on page 146.
Wednesday	**SHOW-AND-TELL DAY WEDNESDAY** **DISCUSSION TOPIC: PEGGY PARISH** Peggy Parish was a teacher. She really understands and appreciates the humor of children. Your classroom will be full of laughter with *Amelia Bedelia*.	**ABOUT PEGGY PARISH** Peggy Parish says that her books are like her children, and she loves them all. She first became interested in stories when she was a very young girl living in South Carolina. She was a sickly child and spent a great deal of time being read to. She just loved sitting and listening to all the stories. As she grew up, she decided that she wanted to be a teacher and taught in Oklahoma and New York. When she began writing, many of her stories were about the history of her home state of South Carolina. She wrote about log cabins and the Indian people. Her most famous character is Amelia Bedelia– a silly maid who takes everything literally.		**READ, *AMELIA BEDELIA'S FAMILY ALBUM*** Talk about all the funny people in Amelia Bedelia's family. Make your own family album. Draw a picture of different family members and then dictate a new name for them. For example, Cousin Katie, the kitten lover. Complete directions are on page 147
Thursday	**DISCUSSION TOPIC: ERIC CARLE** A favorite author of early childhood teachers and children is Eric Carle.	**ABOUT ERIC CARLE** Eric Carle lived in New York but had to move to Germany when he was only 6 years old. He missed his New York friends and had to learn to speak German. Eric did not see his father for 8 years because his father was a prisoner of war during WWII. As Eric grew older, he studied art in Germany. In 1950 he moved back to the United States. He had many jobs there. One of his jobs was illustrating children's books. He found that he liked it so well that he made it his career. A favorite book of his is, *Do You Want to Be My Friend?*		**ERIC CARLE'S ART** Eric Carle uses collages to illustrate his books. Go to a home decorating store and ask for a donation of their old wallpaper sample books. Let the children cut apart the wallpaper and create a picture. **READ, *PANDA BEAR, PANDA BEAR, WHAT DO YOU SEE?*** Complete directions can be found on page 148.
Friday	**SPECIAL NEWS FRIDAY** **DISCUSSION TOPIC: WE CAN BE AUTHORS** The children have had a fun week listening to some great stories and learning about the wonderful authors. Today the children are going to be authors.	**OUR OWN CLASSROOM BIG BOOK** The book will be titled, *Our Favorite Things.* Have the children work in pairs. Each child should draw their favorite thing on an 11" x 17" piece of paper. *(Two drawings on a page.)* On each page write: Our favorites things are a ___ and a ____. Bind together and read together as a class.	**BOOKMARKS AND INCENTIVE CHARTS** On page 149 you will find some reproducible bookmarks and incentive charts for the children to use at home and at school.	**FREQUENT READER'S AWARD PROGRAM** On page 149 you will find a letter to send home to the parents, along with a **"Frequent Reader's Card."** This is a gentle reminder to parents of the importance of reading to their child and a fun incentive program for the children.

One Fish, Two Fish

In this book, Dr. Seuss introduces children to many different opposites.
Match the funny fish opposites. Can you find them in the book, *One Fish, Two Fish?*

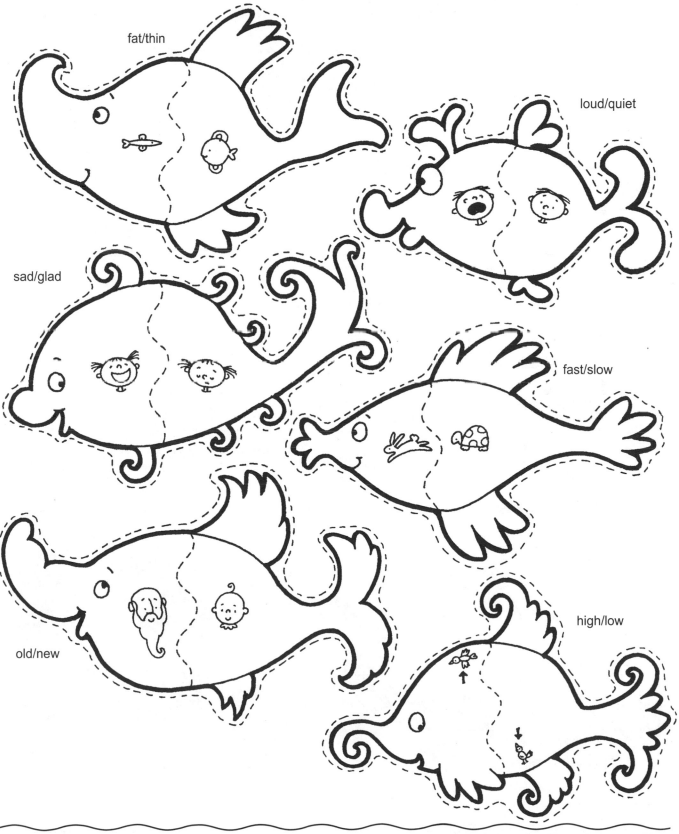

fat/thin

loud/quiet

sad/glad

fast/slow

old/new

high/low

145

The List – Activity from Frog and Toad Together

Directions: *The List* is a short story from Arnold Lobel's book, *Frog and Toad Together*. Toad made a list so he could remember everything that he should do that day. Here are some pictures of Toad and Frog's day. Color the pictures, cut them out, and glue them in the order of the day.

Answer key:
1. Toad wakes up.
2. Toad eats breakfast.
3. Toad gets dressed.
4. Toad goes to Frog's house.
5. Toad and Frog go on a walk.
6. The wind blows the list away.
7. Toad and Frog chase the list.
8. Toad and Frog go to sleep.

Toad wakes up.

Toad eats breakfast.

Toad gets dressed.

Toad goes to Frog's house.

Toad and Frog go on a walk.

The wind blows the list away.

Toad and Frog chase the list.

Toad and Frog go to sleep.

Amelia Bedelia!

After listening to the story, *Amelia Bedelia,* pretend that you are a silly maid and draw what you would do in each box.

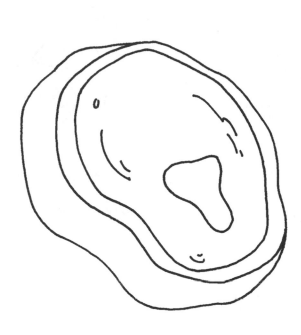

Trim the fat on the meat.

Draw the drapes.

Put the lights out.

Dress the chicken.

Panda Bear, Panda Bear, What Do You See?

Directions: These are the ten animals that appear in the story, *Panda Bear, Panda Bear, What Do You See?* Copy a set of animals for each child. Have the children color the animals and cut them out along the dotted lines. Have the children glue them in order on a large sheet of paper. Let the children take turns retelling the story. Send this home and ask the children to retell the story to their parents.

Answer key: This is the correct order of the story: 1. panda bear 2. bald eagle 3. water buffalo 4. spider monkey 5. green sea turtle 6. macaroni penguin 7. sea lion 8. red wolf 9. whooping crane 10. black panther

panda bear

bald eagle

water buffalo

spider monkey

green sea turtle

macaroni penguin

sea lion

red wolf

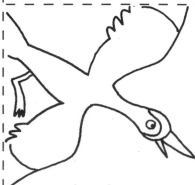
whooping crane

black panther

Frequent Reader's Award Program!

Dear Parents,

This week the children have been learning about some famous children's authors and have heard some wonderful stories. This program is designed to encourage the children to keep up their interest in stories and books.

Please put up the incentive chart on your refrigerator. There are 15 boxes. Each time you read a book to your child, fill in one of the boxes. When the chart is filled, send it to school with your child. Your child will receive a **Story Time Bookmark Award** and I will send home another Frequent Reader's Card.

Developing an interest in books and listening to stories is one of the best activities that we can do to help prepare young children to read. Children who are read to frequently, more often become good readers and grow up loving books!

Thank you, Your child's teacher

Frequent Reader's Card

This Story Time Bookmark Award

is proudly presented to: _____.

Congratulations on completing 15 books!

I LOVE BOOKS !

Theme 31: Who is the Man in the Moon? (Space/Planets/Stars)

	Activity 1	Activity 2	Activity 3	Activity 4
Monday	This week the children are going to talk about outer space, the stars, the moon, the planets, and what it would be like to travel into space. **DISCUSSION TOPIC: WHAT IS OUT THERE IN SPACE?** Make a list with the children of all the things they think are out in space.	**THIS IS WHAT I SEE IN OUTER SPACE!** Copy page 151 for each child. Have them draw a spaceship and whatever else they think they might see. **PATTERN BLOCKS** Use pattern blocks to build images that look like rockets.	**SPACE BANNER** Create a long banner by gluing or taping together 12 sheets of 8.5" x 11" black construction paper. Let the children use white chalk to create stars, plants, and spaceships on the banner. Adding glitter is a fun extra touch.	**COUNTDOWN TO SPACE** Have all the children squat down. Count backwards from 10 to 1 and then say "Blast Off!" On "Blast Off" the children should jump high into the air.
Tuesday	**DISCUSSION TOPIC: THE STARS** Today the children are going to talk about the stars. Teach the children the rhyme, **"Twinkle, Twinkle Little Star,"** and **"Starlight, Star bright. The very first star I see tonight. I wish I may, I wish I might, have the wish I wish tonight."**	**MAKE A CONSTELLATION** Show the children pictures of constellations. Explain that people named the stars and made up stories about them. Give each child a piece of black construction paper and 10 star stickers. *(Glow-in-the-dark star stickers work best.)* Place the stickers anywhere on the paper. Use white chalk to connect the stars into a constellation.	**THE SUN IS A STAR** Teach the children that the sun is a star, too. Some stars are bigger than the sun and some are smaller. Carefully light a candle and have the children watch the flame flicker. This gives the same effect as stars twinkling in the sky.	**STARS IN THE CLASSROOM** Cut a circle from a piece of black construction paper. Poke holes in the paper. Tape the construction paper with the holes in it over the bulb end of a flashlight. Turn the classroom lights off. Turn on the flashlight and direct the light toward a wall. The children will love seeing all the stars in their classroom.
Wednesday	**SHOW-AND-TELL DAY WEDNESDAY** **DISCUSSION TOPIC: THE MOON** It's so much fun to look up into the sky at night and see the moon. Today the children are going to talk about the moon. Ask the children what they think it is like on the moon.	**MOON COOKIES** Purchase a roll of pre-made cookie dough. Follow the package directions when baking. Cut the dough and put on a cookie sheet. Before you bake the cookies, take the rounded end of a spoon and poke a hole in the dough. When the cookies are done, you will see the craters.	**WHAT DO YOU THINK WE WOULD FIND ON THE MOON?** Use the reproducible activity found on page 152. Have the children draw a picture of the things they think they might see on the moon.	**JUMPING ON THE MOON** In outer space there is no gravity. Gravity is what holds us down on Earth so we don't float away. In outer space people can float, jump very high, and leap long distances. Put on some music and have the children pretend that they are in space. They are very light, move very slowly, and can jump very high.
Thursday	**DISCUSSION TOPIC: THE PLANETS** Show the children pictures of all the planets. This is a very difficult concept for young children. Introducing the children to the solar system will lay a foundation for the future.	**SOLAR SYSTEM BULLETIN BOARD** Cut out nine planets. Place them on a bulletin board in the solar system formation. Talk about and name each planet. We live on the planet Earth. Show the children where Earth is in our solar system.	**PLANETS IN ORDER OF SIZE** Make cut outs of the nine planets. It is impossible to size them accurately. When you cut out the planets just make sure that you make the planet Pluto the smallest and the planet Jupiter the largest. Have the children put the planets in order according to size.	**NASA** NASA has a wonderful web site for children. Type in www.NASA.gov. The children will be able to see space, the moon, and all the planets. **THE EARTH** Copy page 153, for each of the children. Have the children color the water blue and the land green.
Friday	**SPECIAL NEWS FRIDAY** **DISCUSSION TOPIC: LET'S GO OFF TO SPACE** Today the children are going to talk about what it might be like to be an astronaut. They will participate in pretend activities about going into space.	**PACKING FOR SPACE** Let's pretend that we are astronauts and are leaving on our first space voyage. Here is our suitcase. *(Bring in a real suitcase).* What should we pack? What do you think we will need?	**POWERED ROCKETS** Let each student decorate a small lunch bag to resemble a rocket. Blow up a long thin balloon, but do not tie the end. Hold the end of the balloon as you place the bag over the balloon and then let the balloon go. The force of the air leaving the balloon will shoot the paper bag rocket up into the air. Children will love this activity.	**WHAT SHOULD WE EAT IN SPACE?** Provide the children with several fun things to sample that are similar to what astronauts eat in space. Dried foods are fun to experiment with: apples, bananas, fruit roll-ups. Put jello or pudding in a plastic sandwich bag that seals tightly. Cut out a corner of the bag and have the children suck out the pudding or Jello™.

This is What I See in Outer Space!
Draw a spaceship and other things that you might see in outer space.

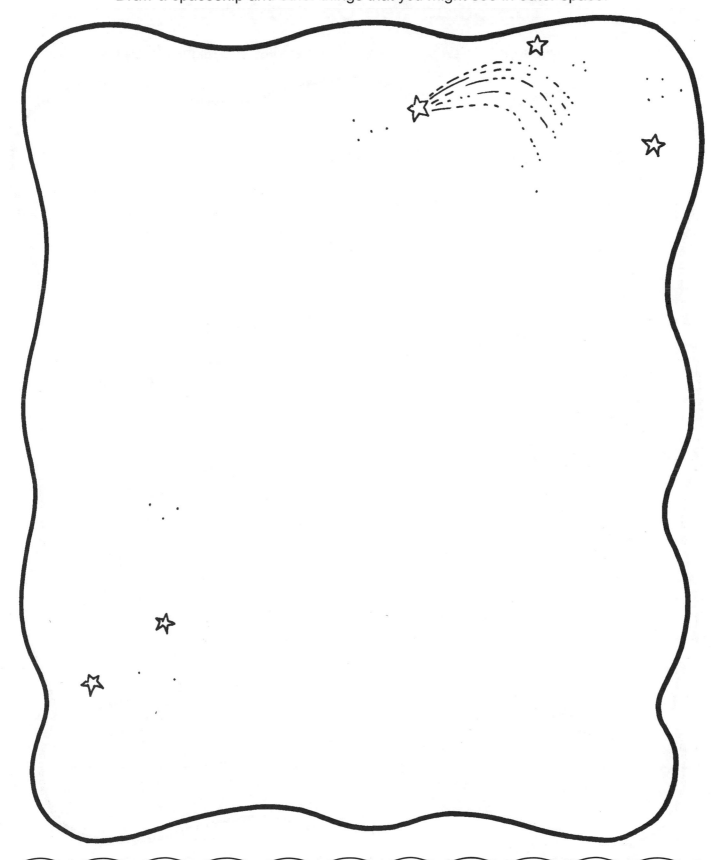

What Do You Think You Could See On The Moon?

This is the moon's surface. Draw some things that you think you might see on the moon.

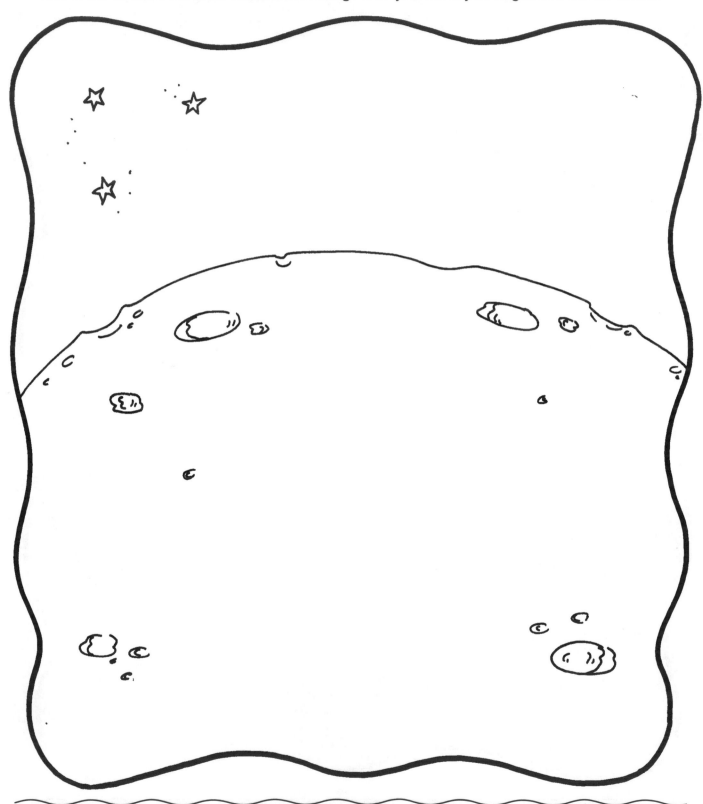

The Earth
Color the water blue and the land green.

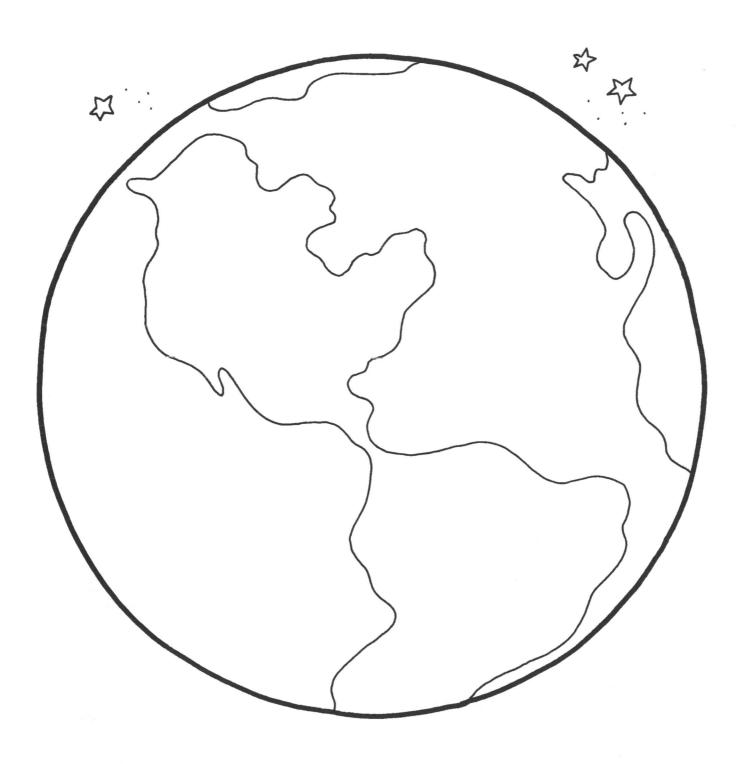

Theme 32: Warm and Watery Days! (Summer Fun)

	Activity 1	Activity 2	Activity 3	Activity 4
Monday	This week the children will celebrate summer, warm weather, and the end of the school year. **DISCUSSION TOPIC: BEACH** Today the children will have fun with beach and sand activities. *Special note to teacher:* Read "The Memory Book–My Year At School" activity and review page 157. You will need to prepare ahead of time for this project. It will be worth it!	**INTERESTING THINGS AT THE BEACH** Set up a table in your classroom with various objects that can be found at the beach or in the water. The children will love to touch and feel these objects: sand, shells, coral, sponges, starfish, sand dollar, sea weed, sharks teeth, and anything else you may be able to locate.	**MAKE A BEACH SCENE** Give each child a piece of light blue card stock. Paint a 2" high strip of white glue along the bottom of the card. Sprinkle sand on the glue. The children have made a beach! If you have any tiny shells, they are a nice addition. If not, draw the sun, the water, and a boat on the water.	**THE PERFECT SUMMER DRINK** There is nothing better than lemonade on a hot summer day. Bring in real lemons and give the children the experience of making (and squeezing) "real" lemonade. Sweeten the lemonade with sugar.
Tuesday	**DISCUSSION TOPIC: FISH AND OTHER SEA LIFE** After the children have discussed the beach, the next obvious topic to talk about are fish and other sea life.	**SEA LIFE BULLETIN BOARD** Cover the bulletin board with light-blue paper. Reproduce the sea life patterns on pages 155–156. Let the children color and cut out the animals. Tape or staple them to the bulletin board. Paint seaweed and other interesting things to the bottom of the bulletin board. Cover the bulletin board with clear plastic wrap to resemble water.	**BLUE JELLO AND FRUIT SNACK SHARKS** Here is an idea for a fun sea food snack. Make blue jello and add shark fruit snacks. The children will think this is a really fun (and silly) snack!	**PET STORE FIELD TRIP** Most pet stores have more fish than any other animal. Arrange a field trip to a local pet store to look at and study the fish. Ask for one of the sales clerks to walk with the children to answer questions.
Wednesday	**SHOW-AND-TELL DAY WEDNESDAY** **DISCUSSION TOPIC: WATER FUN** There is nothing more fun than playing with water when you are a young child. Today the children will participate in some great water activities.	**WATER SAFETY** It is important that young children understand water safety rules. Go over the rules: 1. **NEVER** go near or in the water without an adult being present! 2. **NEVER** push anyone in the water. 3. **NEVER** run by a swimming pool. 4. **ALWAYS** wear a life jacket in a boat.	**READ THE BOOK, *I'M SAFE IN THE WATER*, BY WENDY GORDON** This is a wonderful book that helps children learn not to be afraid of the water. At the same time, it teaches children all about water safety and gives them a true respect for the water.	**SINK AND FLOAT** Fill a small wading pool halfway full with water. Let the children experiment with objects that sink and float. *(The teacher will need to collect these objects before the activity).* Let the children wear swimsuits if possible.
Thursday	**DISCUSSION TOPIC: MORE WATER FUN** Remember running through the sprinklers when you were a young child. Nothing was more fun! Set up sprinklers and let the children experience the thrill of sprinkler fun! Have lots of towels on hand!	**HOW DOES WATER MOVE** This is a fun experiment that visually shows children how water moves. Place a stalk of celery in a glass of colored (food coloring) water. The children will be able to see how the water moves up the celery. You can also divide one stalk of celery into two sections. Place one half in a glass of colored water and the other half in a glass of clear water. Compare the difference.	**FROZEN YOGURT POPS** This is a healthy and tasty treat for the children. Fill an ice cube tray with any kind of yogurt. Place a craft stick in each section before it is completely frozen. When the yogurt is frozen, remove it from the ice tray. The children will love eating their frozen yogurt pops!	**HERMIT CRABS** Hermit crabs are popular pets. The children will be delighted to have a hermit crab in their classroom. They are inexpensive, can be touched by young children, and are fun to watch. Purchase a hermit crab for your classroom—just make sure that you purchase an extra shell. Everytime they grow, they need a new shell!
Friday	**SPECIAL NEWS FRIDAY** **DISCUSSION TOPIC: THE SCHOOL YEAR ENDS** This may be the first year of school for most of the children. Help them make the end of the year memorable!	**THE MEMORY BOOK: MY YEAR AT SCHOOL** This is an incredible project that all the children and parents will treasure. It will require some work on your part. You will need to prepare pages ahead of time for the children. On page 157 you will find a detailed guide that will help you prepare for this activity.		**BANANA ICE CREAM** Cut 3 ripe bananas into large chunks. Beat together the 3 bananas, 12 marshmallows, and 1 tbsp. sugar at high speed for one minute. In another bowl, beat 1 cup of whipping cream until it foams. Fold the whipping cream into the banana mixture and pour into a round cake pan. Cover with foil and freeze. YUM!

Sea Life Patterns

Directions are found on page 154.

Sea Life Patterns

Directions are found on page 154.

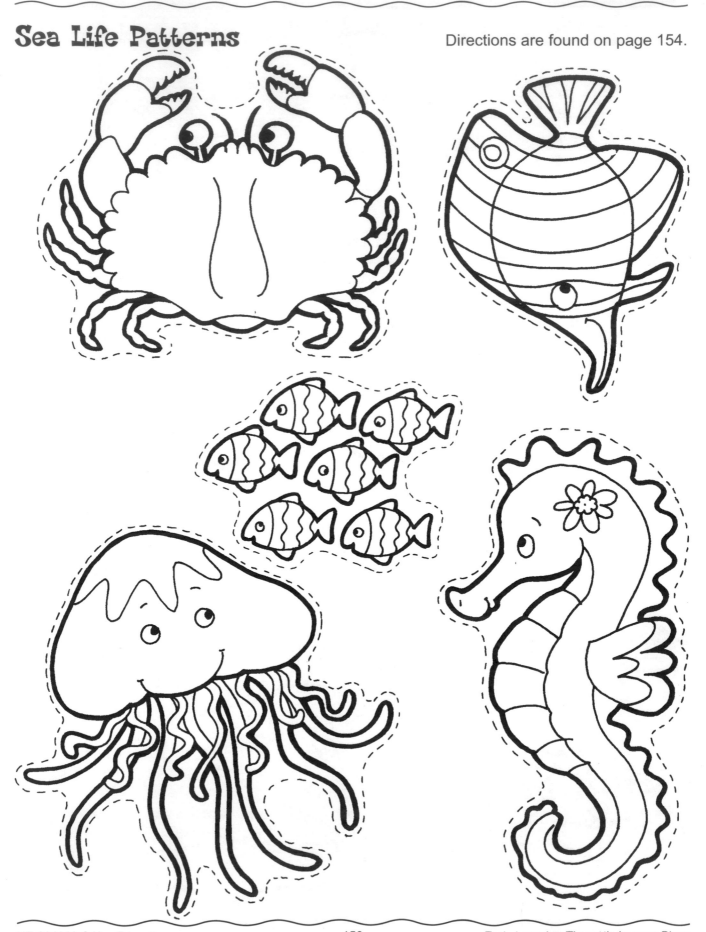

My Memory Book—My Year at School

Use the following guidelines to create nine pages for your student's memory books. Add your own ideas!

**My Memory Book
My Year At School**

The children can
decorate their
own individual
cover designs.

PAGE 1

This was my teacher.

Find a picture of yourself
and make a black and white
photocopy for each child.
The children can paste it into their book.
Write each child a special message.

PAGE 2

We Went On Field Trips

On the top half,
write a list of all the field trips
your class went on this year.

At the bottom of the page, provide a
frame for the children to draw
their favorite field trip.

PAGE 3

**We Learned Rhymes
and Finger Plays**

Fill this page with
your classroom's favorite rhymes
and finger plays.

PAGE 4

We Listened to Stories

Write a list of some of the children's
favorite books that you read
to them this year.
Make a box for the children
to illustrate their favorite book.

PAGE 5

We Learned Songs

Fill this page with
the words to some
of your classroom's
favorite songs.

PAGE 6

We Made Good Treats

Fill this page with the recipes
of some of the foods that were
made in class this year.
Make a box so the children
can draw pictures of themselves
eating their favorite food.

PAGE 7

**This is me!
Look how much I have
grown this year!**

The children draw
their own portraits!

I had a great year!

PAGE 8

**These were my
good friends!**

Let all the children
autograph each other's books.
They should print their names.

PAGE 9

Children's Literature Reference Guide

Theme 1:
Great News! School Begins! *(Getting Acquainted!)*
- *Clifford's First Day at School* by Norman Bridwell. Published by Scholastic, © 1999.
- *If You Take A Mouse to School* by Laura Numeroff. Published by Laura Geringer, © 2002.
- *I Love You All Day Long* by Francesca Rusackas. Published by HarperCollins, © 2002.
- *Miss Bindergarten Gets Ready for Kindergarten* by Joseph Slate, Ashley Wolff. Published by Puffin Books, © 1996.
- *What to Expect at Preschool* by Heidi Murkoff. Published by HarperFestival, © 2001.

Theme 2:
These People Belong to Me! *(Families)*
- *All Families Are Different* by Sol Gordon, Vivien Cohen. Published by Prometheus Books, © 2000.
- *Clifford's Family* by Norman Bridwell. Published by Scholastic, © 1984.
- *Who's in Your Family?* by Robert Skutch, Laura Nienhaus. Published by Tricycle Press, © 1997.

Theme 3:
Where Do You Live? *(Homes)*
- *City Mouse Country Mouse* by John Wallner. Published by Scholastic, © 1987.
- *Corduroy* by Don Freeman. Published by Viking Books, © 1968.
- *In the Country: Follow the Lost Little Rabbit (Little Windows).* Published by DK Publishing, Inc., © 2003.
- *Owl at Home* by Arnold Lobel. Published by HarperTrophy, © 1975.
- *The Tale of Peter Rabbit* by Beatrix Potter. Published by Frederick Warne and Company, © 1987 (original © 1903).

Theme 4:
Apples! Apples! Apples! *(Beginning the School Year)*
- *Apples* by Gail Gibbons. Published by Holiday House, © 2000.
- *How Do Apples Grow?* by Betsy Maestro. Published by HarperTrophy, © 1993.
- *Johnny Appleseed* by Steven Kellogg. Published by HarperCollins, © 1988.
- *The Story of Johnny Appleseed* by Aliki. Published by Aladdin, © 1971.

Theme 5:
Who Works in Your Neighborhood? *(Community Helpers)*
- *A Day with a Mail Carrier* by Jan Kottke. Published by Children's Press, © 2000.
- *Community Helpers from A to Z* by Bobbie Kalmon, Niki Walker. Published by Crabtree Publishing Company, © 1997.
- *I Want to Be a Firefighter* by Dan Liebman. Published by Firefly Books LTD., © 1999.
- *Jobs People Do* by Christopher Maynard. Published by DK Publishing, Inc., © 2001.
- *Maisy Drives the Bus* by Lucy Cousins. Published by Candlewick Press, © 2000.
- *Officer Buckle and Gloria* by Peggy Rathman. Published by Putnam Publishing Group, © 1995.

Theme 6:
Autumn is a Colorful Time! *(Autumn)*
- *Miss Suzy* by Arnold Lobel, Miriam Young. Published by Atheneum, © 1964.
- *Red Leaf, Yellow Leaf* by Lois Ehlert. Published by Harcourt Children's Books, © 1991.
- *Why Do Leaves Change Color?* by Betsy Maestro. Published by HarperTrophy, © 1994.

Theme 7:
It's Harvest Time *(Seeds and Harvesting)*
- *Autumn Harvest* by Alvin R. Tressel, Roger Duvosin. Published by Mulberry Books, © 1990.
- *Harvest Home* by Jane Yolen. Published by Silver Whistle, © 2002.
- *Hello Harvest Moon* by Ralph Fletcher. Published by Clarion Books, © 2003.
- *Scarecrow* by Cynthia Rylant. Published by Voyager Books, © 2001.

Theme 8:
Let's Pretend! *(Pumpkin Fun)*
- *Bats* by Gail Gibbons. Published by Holiday House, © 2000.
- *Good Night Owl* by Pat Hutchins. Published by Simon & Schuster Children's Publishing, © 1972.
- *It's the Great Pumpkin, Charlie Brown* by Charles Schultz. Published by Random House Books for Young Readers, © 1980.
- *Pumpkin Soup* by Helen Cooper. Published by Farrar, Strauss and Giroux, © 1999.
- *The Owl and the Pussycat* by Edward Lear. Published by Bedrick, © 1993.
- *Too Many Pumpkins* by Linda White, Megan Lloyd. Published by Holiday House, © 1997.
- *Zipping, Zapping, Zooming Bats* by Ann Earle. Published by HarperTrophy, © 1995.

Theme 9:
People Move in Many Ways *(Transportation)*
- *Choo-Choo* by Virginia Lee Burton. Published by Houghton Mifflin, © 1988.
- *Curious George and the Dump Truck* by H.A. Rey. Published by Houghton Mifflin, © 1999.
- *I Stink!* by Kate McMullan. Published by Joanna Cotler, © 2002.
- *Katy and the Big Snow* by Virginia Lee Burton. Published by Houghton Mifflin, © 1974.
- *The Little Engine that Could* by Watty Piper, George Hauman, Doris Hauman. Published by Penguin Books for Young Readers, © 1978.

Theme 10:
Those Magic Words *(Manners)*
- *The Berenstain Bears and the Truth* by Stan and Jan Berenstain. Published by Random House, © 1983.
- *Clifford's Manners* by Norman Bridwell. Published by Scholastic, © 1987.
- *Excuse Me!: A Little Book of Manners* by Karen Katz. Published by Grosset & Dunlap, © 2002.
- *Share and Take Turns (Learning to Get Along)* by Cheri Meiners. Published by Free Spirit Publishing, © 2003.
- *Sharing is Fun* by Joanna Cole. Published by HarperCollins, © 2004.

Theme 11:
I Am Grateful *(Thanksgiving)*
- *The Night Before Thanksgiving* by Natasha Wing, Tammie Lyon. Published by Grosset & Dunlap, © 2001.
- *Thanksgiving: A Harvest Celebration* by Julie Stiegemeyer, Renne Benoit. Published by Concordia Publishing House, © 2003.
- *Thanksgiving is for Giving Thanks* by Margaret Sutherland, Sonja Lamut. Published by Grosset & Dunlap, © 2000.
- *The Very First Thanksgiving Day* by Rhonda Gowler Greene, Susan Gaber. Published by Atheneum, © 2002.

Theme 12:
It's A Colorful World! *(Colors)*
- *A Color of His Own* by Leo Lionni. Published by Scholastic, © 1975.

- *Babar's Book of Color* by Laurent De Brunoff. Published by Harry A. Abrams, © New edition 2004.
- *Brown Bear, Brown Bear, What Do You See?* by Bill Martin, Eric Carle. Published by Henry Holt, © 1996.
- *Cat's Colors* by Jane Cabrera. Published by Puffin Books, © 2000.
- *The Crayola Rainbow Colors Book* by Salina Yoon. Published by Little Simon, © 2004.
- *Mouse Paint* by Ellen Stoll Walsh. Published by Red Wagon Books, © 1995.
- *My Many Colored Days* by Dr. Seuss. Published by Knopf Books for Young Readers, © 1996.

Theme 13:
So Many Holidays! *(December Holidays)*
- *Burro and the Basket* by Lloyd Mardis, Scott Arbuckle. Published by Eakin Press, © 1997.
- *Christmas Around the World* by Mary D. Lankford. Published by HarperTrophy, © 1998.
- *Festival of Lights: The Story of Hanukkah* by Marda Silverman. Published by Aladdin, © 1999.
- *Going Home* by Eve Bunting. Published by Joanna Cotler, © 1996.
- *Hershel and the Hanukkah Goblins* by Eric Kimmel, Trina Schart Hyman. Published by Holiday House, © 1994.
- *Kwanzaa: A Celebration of Family, Community, and Culture.* Published by University of Sank Ore Press, © 1997.
- *Legend of the Poinsettia* by Tomie de Paola. Published by Putnam Publishing Group, © 1997.
- *The Night of Las Posadas* by Tomie de Paola. Published by Putnam Publishing Group, © 1999.
- *The Polar Express* by Chris Van Allsburg. Published by Houghton Mifflin, © 1985.

Theme 14:
It's Cold Out There! *(Winter)*
- *Amazing Arctic Animals* by Jackie Glassman, Lisa Bonforte. Published by Grosset & Dunlap, © 2002.
- *The Mitten* by Jan Brett. Published by Putnam Publishing Group, © 1989.
- *On Mother's Lap* by Ann Herbert Scott. Published by Clarion Books, © 1992.
- *Polar Bear, Polar Bear, What Do you Hear?* by Bill Martin, Eric Carle. Published by Henry Holt & Co., © 1997.
- *The Snowman* by Raymond Biggs. Published by Random House Children's Publishing, © 1989.
- *The Tomten* by Astrid Lindgren, Harald Wiberg, Viktor Rydberg. Published by PaperStar Books, © 1997.

Theme 15:
I Am Healthy *(Nutrition and Health)*
- *Bear Loves Food* by Janelle Cherrington. Published by Simon Spotlight, © 1999.
- *Calling Dr. Amelia Bedelia* by Herman Parish. Published by Greenwillow Press, © 2002.
- *Doctor De Soto* by William Steig. Published by Scholastic, © 1986.
- *From Head to Toe* by Eric Carle. Published by HarperTrophy, © 1999.
- *Going to the Doctor* by T. Berry Brazelton, Alfred Womack, Sam Ogden. Published by Perseus Books, © 1996.
- *Pooh and Friends Exercise Pack (Healthy Kids).* Published by Studio Mouse, © 2004.
- *The Tooth Book* by Theo LeSieg, Joseph Matthew, Dr. Seuss. Published by Random House, © 2000.

Theme 16:
I Care About You *(Valentine's Day)*
- *Do You Want to Be My Friend?* by Eric Carle. Published by HarperTrophy, © 1987.
- *Guess How Much I Love You* by Sam McBratney, Anita Jeram. Published by Candlewick Press, © 1996.
- *I Love My Mama* by Peter Kavanagh. Published by Simon & Schuster Children's Publishing, © 2003.
- *McDuff's New Friends* by Rosemary Wells. Published by Hyperion Books for Children, © 1998.
- *The Valentine Mice* by Bethany Roberts, Doug Cushman. Published by Clarion Books, © 1997.
- *Who Will Be My Friends?* by Syd Hoff. Published by HarperTrophy, © 1985.

Theme 17:
The Shapes of Things *(Shapes)*
- *Color Zoo Board Book* by Lois Ehlert. Published by HarperFestival, © 1997.
- *Raggety Ann and Andy: I Spy! A Book of Shapes* by Patricia Hall. Published by Little Simon, © 2001.
- *The Shape of Me & Other Stuff* by Dr. Seuss. Published by Random House Books for Young Readers, © 1973.
- *The Shape of Things* by Dayle Ann Dodds, Julie Lacome. Published by Candlewick Press, © 1996.
- *So Many Circles, So Many Squares* by Tana Hoban. Published by Greenwillow Press, © 1998.

Theme 18:
Somewhere Over The Rainbow *(St. Patrick's Day)*
- *Jack and the Leprechaun* by Ivan Robertson. Published by Random House Books for Young Readers, © 2000.
- *The Rainbow Fish* by Marcus Pfister, J. Alison James. Published by Nord-Sud Verlag, © 1992.
- *A Rainbow of My Own* by Don Freeman. Published by Puffin Books, © 1978.
- *St. Patrick's Day* by Gail Gibbons. Published by Holiday House, © 1995.
- *St. Patrick's Day In the Morning* by Eve Bunting. Published by Clarion Books, © 1983.

Theme 19:
The Greatest Show On Earth *(Circus)*
- *Circus* by Jack Prelutsky, Arnold Lobel. Published by MacMillian Publishing Company, © 1974.
- *If I Ran the Circus!* by Dr. Seuss. Published by Random House Books for Young Readers, © 1956.
- *Harold's Circus* by Crockett Johnson. Published by HarperTrophy, © 1981.
- *See the Circus* by H.A. Rey. Published by Houghton Mifflin, © 1998.
- *Spot Goes to the Circus* by Eric Hill. Published by Puffin Books, © 1994.

Theme 20:
Let's Go Fly A Kite! *(Weather)*
- *I Love You Sun, I Love You Moon* by Karen Pandell, Tomie de Paola. Published by Putnam Publishing Group, © 1994.
- *Rain* by Robert Kaplan. Published by HarperTrophy, © 1991.
- *Rain Drop Splash* by Alvin Tresselt. Published by HarperTrophy, © 1990.
- *The Wind Blew* by Pat Hutchins. Published by Alladdin, © 1993.

Theme 21:
Things That Make Me Feel Good *(Self-Esteem)*
- *All About Me* by Melanie Gerth, Mary Theien. Published by Piggy Toes Press, © 2000.
- *Babies* by G. Fujikawa. Published by Grosset & Dunlap, © 1977.
- *Stand Tall, Molly Lou Melon* by Patty Lovell, David Catrow. Published by GP Putnam's Sons, © 2001.
- *Tell Me Something Happy Before I Go To Sleep* by Joyce Dunbar, Debi Gliori. Published by Harcourt Children's Books, © 1998.
- *Tell Me What It's Like to Be Big* by Joyce Dunbar. Published by Harcourt Children's Books, © 2001.

Theme 22:
We Love Mother Goose! *(Nursery Rhymes)*
- *Mother Goose: The Children's Classic Edition* by Leon Baxter, Graham Perry, Gary Rees, Kay Widdowson, Jenny Williams. Published by Running Press Book Publishers, © 1997
- *My Very First Mother Goose* by Rosemary Wells, Iona Archibald. Published by Candlewick Press, © 1996.
- *Read Aloud Rhymes for the Very Young* by Jack Prelutsky. Published by Knopf Books for Children, © 1997.

Theme 23:
What Grows in the Garden? *(Planting/Spring)*
- *The Carrot Seed* by Ruth Krauss, Crockett Johnson. Published by HarperCollins, © 1993.
- *The Gigantic Turnip* by Aleksei Tolstoy, Niamh Sharkey. Published by Barefoot Books, © 1999.
- *Growing Vegetable Soup* by Lois Ehlert. Published by Voyager Books, © 1990.
- *Maisy's Garden* by Lucy Cousins. Published by Candlewick Press, © 2001.
- *Planting a Rainbow* by Lois Ehlert. Published by Voyager Press, © 1992.

Theme 24:
Who Says, "Moo," "Quack," and "Oink?" *(The Farm)*
- *All The Places To Love* by Patricia MacLachlan. Published by HarperCollins, © 1994.
- *Click, Clack, Moo: Cows That Type* by Doreen Cronin. Published by Simon & Schuster Children's Publishing, © 2000.
- *Farming* by Gail Gibbons. Published by Holiday House, © 1990.
- *Giggle, Giggle, Quack* by Doreen Cronin. Published by Simon & Schuster Children's Publishing, © 2002.
- *Old MacDonald Had A Farm* by Carol Jones. Published by Houghton Mifflin/Walter Lorraine Books, © 1998.
- *Our Animal Friends at Maple Hill Farm* by Alice Provensen. Published by Sagebrush Bound, © 2000.

Theme 25:
Bugs, Beetles, and Other Creepy, Crawly Things *(Insects)*
- *Five Green and Speckled Frogs* by Priscilla Burris. Published by Cartwheel Books, © 2003.
- *Frog and Toad All Year Long* by Arnold Lobel. Published by HarperCollins, © 1976.
- *Miss Spider's Sunny Patch Kids* by David Kirk. Published by Scholastic, © 2004.
- *The Very Busy Spider* by Eric Carle. Published by Philomel Books, © 1995.
- *The Very Hungry Caterpillar* by Eric Carle. Published by Philomel Books, © 1994.
- *The Very Lonely Firefly* by Eric Carle. Published by Philomel Books, © 1999.

Theme 26:
Early Childhood Olympics *(Staying Fit)*
- *Let the Games Begin* by Maya Ajmera, Michael Regan, Bill Bradley, Shakti for the Children's Organization. Published by Charlesbridge Publishing, © 2000.
- *Olympics!* by B.J. Hennesey, Michael Chatsworth. Published by Puffin Books, © 2000.
- *Stop! The Watch: A Book of Everyday, Ordinary, Anybody Olympics.* Published by Klutz Press, © 1993.

Theme 27:
Growl! Roar! *(Jungle Animals)*
- *The Ant and The Elephant* by Bill Peet. Published by Houghton Mifflin, © 1980.
- *Caps for Sale* by Esphyr Slobodkina. Published by HarperTrophy, © 1987.

- *Curious George* by H. A. Rey. Published by Houghton Mifflin, © 1973.
- *Giraffes Can't Dance* by Giles Andreae, Gary Parker-Rees. Published by Scholastic, © 2001.
- *Lyle, Lyle Crocodile* by Bernard Waber. Published by Houghton Mifflin/Walter Lorraine Books, © 1973.
- *The Story of Babar* by Jean De Brunhoff. Published by Random House Books for Young Readers, © 1937.

Theme 28:
We Are Proud of Our Country! *(Citizenship/Patriotism)*
- *Anno's USA* by Mitsumasa Anno. Published by Philomel Books, © 1983.
- *Caillou What's That Noise?* by Marion Johnson. Published by Chouette Editions, © 2004.
- *The Canada Geese Quilt* by Natalie Kinsey-Warnock, Leslie Bowman. Published by Puffin Books, © 2000.
- *Patriotism* by Lucia Raatma, Madonna Murphy. Published by Bridgestone Books, © 2000.

Theme 29:
Furry Family Members! *(Pets)*
- *Arthur's Pet Business* by Marc Brown. Published by Little Brown, © 1993.
- *Bittle* by Patricia and Emily MacLachlan. Published by Joanna Cotler, © 2004.
- *How to Talk to Your Cat* by Jean Craighead George. Published by HarperCollins, © 2000.
- *How to Talk to Your Dog* by Jean Craighead George. Published by HarperCollins, © 2000.
- *I'll Always Love You* by Hans Wilhelm. Published by Dragonfly Books, © 1998.
- *Pet Show* by Ezra Jack Keats. Published by Puffin Books, © 2001.

Theme 30:
Read Me A Story! *(Building Literacy)*
- *Recommended books can be found on lesson plan page 144.*

Theme 31:
Who is the Man in the Moon? *(Space/Planets/Stars)*
- *The Moon Book* by Gail Gibbons. Published by Holiday House, © 1998.
- *The Planets* by Gail Gibbons. Published by Holiday House, © 1994.
- *Stars: A New Way to See Them* by H. A. Rey. Published by Houghton Mifflin, © 1976.
- *Twinkle, Twinkle Little Star* by Jane Taylor, Slyvia Long. Published by Chronicle Books, © 2001.

Theme 32:
Warm and Watery Days *(Summer Fun)*
- *Beach Day* by Karen Roosa. Published by Clarion Books, © 2001.
- *Curious George at the Beach* by H A. Rey. Published by Houghton Mifflin, © 1988.
- *How to Hide an Octopus and Other Sea Creatures* by Ruth Heller. Published by Grosset & Dunlap, © 1992.
- *On My Beach There Are Many Pebbles* by Leo Lionni. Published by HarperTrophy, © 1995.
- *A Swim Through the Sea* by Kristin Joy Pratt. Published by Dawn Publications, © 1994.
- *Ten Little Fish* by Audrey Wood. Published by Blue Sky Press, © 2004.